ECONOMIC ISSUES, PROBLEMS AND PERSPECTIVES

FEDERAL BUDGET BREAKDOWNS BY SUPERFUNCTIONS AND SUBFUNCTIONS

SELECT ANALYSES

Economic Issues, Problems and Perspectives

Additional books in this series can be found on Nova's website under the Series tab.

Additional E-books in this series can be found on Nova's website under the e-books tab.

American Political, Economic, and Security Issues

Additional books in this series can be found on Nova's website under the Series tab.

Additional E-books in this series can be found on Nova's website under the e-books tab.

ECONOMIC ISSUES, PROBLEMS AND PERSPECTIVES

FEDERAL BUDGET BREAKDOWNS BY SUPERFUNCTIONS AND SUBFUNCTIONS

SELECT ANALYSES

SIMON F. MATHIS
AND
IVORY B. HEWITT
EDITORS

Nova Science Publishers, Inc.
New York

For permission to use material from this book please contact us:
Telephone 631-231-7269; Fax 631-231-8175
Web Site: http://www.novapublishers.com

Library of Congress Cataloging-in-Publication Data

ISBN: 978-1-62081-048-4

Published by Nova Science Publishers, Inc. † New York

CONTENTS

PREFACE

Discussions about the appropriate levels of spending for various policy objectives of the federal government have played an important role in congressional deliberations over funding measures for FY2011, and are expected to play a central role as Congress considers decisions affecting the FY2012 budget. This book provides a graphical overview of historical trends in discretionary budget authority from 1976-2010, with estimates for 2011 spending, and the levels consistent with President Obama's proposals for 2012-2016.

Chapter 1- President Obama's FY2012 budget submission was released on February 14, 2011. This report provides a graphical overview of historical trends in discretionary budget authority (BA) from FY1976 through FY2010, estimates for FY2011 spending, and the levels consistent with the President's proposals for FY2012 through FY2016.

Discussions about the appropriate levels of spending for various policy objectives of the federal government have played an important role in congressional deliberations over funding measures for FY2011, and are expected to play a central role as Congress considers decisions affecting the FY2012 budget. As the 112th Congress considers funding levels for FY2011, FY2012, and beyond, past spending trends may prove useful in framing policy discussions. For example, rapid growth in national defense and other security spending in the past decade has played an important role in fiscal discussions. The sharp increases in federal spending on education, energy, and other areas funded by the American Recovery and Reinvestment Act of have been noted in recent budget debates. This report may provide a starting point for discussions about spending trends and federal priorities, but it does not attempt to explain spending patterns in each policy area. Other CRS products, however, can provide insights into those spending trends in specific functional areas.

Chapter 2- The 112th Congress is focusing attention on short- and long-term efforts to reduce the federal deficit and stabilize the national debt, including proposals to alter the overall size and composition of total federal spending. Components of the federal budget categorized as "human resources" account for the majority of federal outlays (70% in FY2010) and would be affected by these proposals. Six functional categories comprise the human resources "superfunction": education, training, employment, and social services; health (primarily Medicaid); Medicare; income security; Social Security; and veterans benefits and services.

President Obama submitted a detailed FY2012 budget request to Congress on February 14, and in April, he released a set of deficit reduction policies intended to build on the February proposal called the *President's Framework for Shared Prosperity and Shared Fiscal Responsibility*. On April 15, the House passed a concurrent resolution on the FY2012 budget (H.Con.Res. 34) that was based on a document called *Path to Prosperity,* released by Budget Committee Chairman Paul Ryan on April 5. The Senate has not yet acted on a budget resolution for FY2012.

In: Federal Budget Breakdowns ... ISBN: 978-1- 62081-048-4
Editors: S. F. Mathis and I .B. Hewitt

Chapter 1

DISCRETIONARY BUDGET AUTHORITY BY SUBFUNCTION: AN OVERVIEW*

D. Andrew Austin

SUMMARY

President Obama's FY2012 budget submission was released on February 14, 2011. This report provides a graphical overview of historical trends in discretionary budget authority (BA) from FY1976 through FY2010, estimates for FY2011 spending, and the levels consistent with the President's proposals for FY2012 through FY2016.

Discussions about the appropriate levels of spending for various policy objectives of the federal government have played an important role in congressional deliberations over funding measures for FY2011, and are expected to play a central role as Congress considers decisions affecting the FY2012 budget. As the 112th Congress considers funding levels for FY2011, FY2012, and beyond, past spending trends may prove useful in framing policy discussions. For example, rapid growth in national defense and other security spending in the past decade has played an important role in fiscal discussions. The sharp increases in federal spending on education, energy, and other areas funded by the American Recovery and Reinvestment Act of 2009 (ARRA; P.L. 111-5) have been noted in recent budget debates. This report may provide

---

* This is an edited, reformatted and augmented version of the Congressional Research Service Publication, CRS Report for Congress R41726, dated March 29, 2011.

a starting point for discussions about spending trends and federal priorities, but it does not attempt to explain spending patterns in each policy area. Other CRS products, however, can provide insights into those spending trends in specific functional areas.

Functional categories (e.g., national defense, agriculture, etc.) provide a means to compare federal funding for activities within broad policy areas that often cut across several federal agencies. Subfunction categories provide a finer division of funding levels within narrower policy areas. Budget function categories are used within the budget resolution and for other purposes, such as possible program cuts and tax expenditures.

The report includes a series of figures showing discretionary budget authority as a percentage of gross domestic product (GDP), which compares spending levels in each functional category with the size of the U.S. economy. Measuring spending as a percentage of GDP in effect controls for inflation and population increases. A flat line on such graphs indicates that spending in that category is increasing at the same rate as overall economic growth.

Three functions, however, are omitted. These are (1) allowances, which contain items reflecting technical budget adjustments; (2) net interest, which by its nature is not discretionary spending; and (3) undistributed offsetting receipts, which are treated for federal budgetary purposes as negative budget authority.

Spending in this report is measured in terms of discretionary budget authority as a percentage of GDP. Discretionary spending is provided and controlled through appropriations acts, which fund many of the activities commonly associated with such federal government functions as running executive branch agencies, congressional offices and agencies, and international operations of the government. Essentially all spending on federal wages and salaries is discretionary. Program administration costs for entitlement programs such as Social Security, is generally funded by discretionary spending, while mandatory spending generally funds the benefits provided through those programs. Thus, the figures showing trends in discretionary budget authority presented herein do not reflect the much larger expenditures on program benefits supported by mandatory spending. For some federal agencies, such as the Departments of Veterans Affairs and Transportation, the division of expenditures into discretionary and mandatory categories can be complex. This report will not be updated.

This report presents figures showing trends in discretionary budget authority as a percentage of GDP by subfunction within each of 17 budget function categories, using data from President Obama's FY2012 budget submission.[1] Discretionary spending is provided and controlled through appropriations acts, which fund many of the activities commonly associated with such federal government functions as running executive branch agencies, congressional offices and agencies, and international operations of the government.[2] Discretionary spending in this report is measured in terms of budget authority. Budget authority for an agency has been compared to having funds in a checking account. Funds are available, subject to congressional restrictions, and can be used to enter into obligations such as contracts or hiring personnel. Outlays occur when the U.S. Treasury disburses funds to honor those obligations. Measuring spending as a percentage of GDP in effect controls for inflation and population increases. A flat line on such graphs indicates that spending in that category is increasing at the same rate as overall economic growth.

Discussions about the appropriate levels of spending for various policy objectives of the federal government have played an important role in congressional deliberations over funding measures for FY2011, and are expected to play a central role as Congress considers decisions affecting the FY2012 budget. As the 112th Congress considers funding levels for FY2011, FY2012, and beyond, past spending trends may prove useful in framing policy discussions. For example, rapid growth in national defense and other security spending in the past decade has played an important role in fiscal discussions. The sharp increases in federal spending on education, energy, and other areas funded by The American Recovery and Reinvestment Act of 2009 (ARRA; P.L. 111-5) have also played a significant role in recent budget debates.

This report provides a graphical overview of historical trends in discretionary budget authority from FY1976 through FY2010, estimates for FY2011 spending, and the levels consistent with the President's proposals for FY2012 through FY2016.[3] Budget data for FY2011 in the FY2012 budget documents represent annualized levels reflecting funding levels in the continuing resolution (P.L. 111-242) that provided discretionary funding until March 4, 2011.[4] Subsequent adjustments to funding levels are not reflected in data or figures presented in this report.[5] Trends in net interest are excluded as federal interest expenditures have been automatically appropriated since 1847. Allowances, which contain items reflecting technical budget adjustments, and undistributed offsetting receipts are also excluded.

Figures in this report are based on the Office of Management and Budget (OMB) Public Budget Database accompanying the FY2012 budget release.[6] Table 5.1 in the *Historical Tables* volume of the FY2012 budget reports budget authority by function and subfunction, but does not provide a breakdown by discretionary and mandatory subcomponents.[7]

OMB is generally regarded as the official custodian of historical federal budget data. While OMB has attempted to make these data consistent, changes in government accounting standards and agency reorganizations, among other changes, may raise difficulties in comparing data from different fiscal years. In addition, OMB data may not reflect certain zero-balance transfers among funds, which may play an important role in the funding of some federal programs.

BACKGROUND ON FUNCTIONAL CATEGORIES

Functional categories provide a means to compare federal funding for activities within broad policy areas that often cut across several federal agencies.[8] Because various federal agencies may have closely related or overlapping responsibilities, and because some agencies have responsibilities in diverse policy areas, budget data divided along functional categories can provide a useful view of federal activities in support of specific national purposes.

Superfunction categories, which provide a higher level division of federal activities, are

- National defense,
- Human resources,
- Physical resources,
- Other functions,
- Net interest,
- Allowances, and
- Undistributed offsetting receipts.

Superfunction categories for national defense, net interest, allowances, and undistributed offsetting receipts coincide with function categories.

Budget function categories, grouped by superfunctions, are shown in **Table 1**. Subfunction categories provide a finer division of funding levels within narrower policy areas.

Subsequent figures follow the ordering of functions in **Table 1**.

Table 1. Budget Function Categories by Superfunction

Superfunction	Code	Function (Subfunction)
National Defense	50	**National defense**
	51	Dept. of Defense-Military
	53	Atomic energy defense activities
	54	Defense-related activities
Human Resources	500	**Education, training, employment, and social services**
	501	Elementary, secondary, and vocational educ.
	502	Higher education
	503	Research and general education aids
	504	Training and employment
	505	Other labor services
	506	Social services
	550	**Health**
	551	Health care services
	552	Health research and training
	554	Consumer and occupational health and safety
	570	**Medicare**
	571	Medicare
	600	**Income security**
	601	Gen. retirement & disab. insurance (exc. Soc. Sec.)
	602	Federal employee retirement and disability
	603	Unemployment compensation
	604	Housing assistance
	605	Food and nutrition assistance
	609	Other income security
	650	**Social security**
	651	Social security
	700	**Veterans benefits and services**
	701	Income security for veterans
	702	Veterans education, training, & rehab.
	703	Hospital and medical care for veterans
	704	Veterans housing
	705	Other veterans benefits and services

Table 1. (Continued)

Superfunction	Code	Function (Subfunction)
Physical Resources	270	**Energy**
	271	Energy supply
	272	Energy conservation
	274	Emergency energy preparedness
	276	Energy information, policy, and regulation
	300	**Natural resources and environment**
	301	Water resources
	302	Conservation and land mgmt.
	303	Recreational resources
	304	Pollution control and abatement
	306	Other natural resources
	370	**Commerce and housing credit**
	371	Mortgage credit
	372	Postal service
	373	Deposit insurance
	376	Other advancement of commerce
	400	**Transportation**
	401	Ground transportation
	402	Air transportation
	403	Water transportation
	407	Other transportation
	450	**Community and regional development**
	451	Community dev.
	452	Area and regional dev.
	453	Disaster relief and insurance
Other Functions	150	**International affairs**
	151	Intl. dev. and humanitarian assistance
	152	Intl. security assistance
	153	Conduct of foreign affairs
	154	Foreign information & exchange activities
	155	Intl. financial programs
	250	**General science, space, and technology**
	251	General science and basic research
	252	Space flight, research & supporting activities
	350	**Agriculture**
	351	Farm income stabilization
	352	Agricultural research and services

Superfunction	Code	Function (Subfunction)
	750	**Administration of justice**
	751	Federal law enforcement activities
	752	Federal litigative and judicial activities
	753	Federal correctional activities
	754	Criminal justice assistance
	800	**General government**
	801	Legislative functions
	802	Executive direction and mgmt.
	803	Central fiscal operations
	804	General property and records mgmt.
	805	Central personnel mgmt.
	806	General purpose fiscal assistance
	808	Other general government
	809	Deductions for offsetting receipts
Net Interest	900	**Net interest**
	901	Interest on Treasury debt securities (gross)
	902	Interest received by on-budget trust funds
	903	Interest received by off-budget trust funds
	908	Other interest
	909	Other Investment and income
Allowances	920	**Allowances**
	925	Future Disaster Costs
	926	Offset to Medicare SGR Costs
	929	Adjustment to reach FY2011 Bud Request
Undistributed Offsetting Receipts	950	**Undistributed offsetting receipts**
	951	Employer share, employee retirement (on-budget)
	952	Employer share, employee retirement (off-budget)
	953	Rents & royalties on the Outer Continental Shelf
	954	Sale of major assets
	959	Other undistributed offsetting receipts

Source: CRS, based on OMB data.

Note: Allowances subfunctions may change from year to year.

DISCRETIONARY SPENDING IN THE FY2012 BUDGET

President Obama, in his FY2012 budget, proposed extending a three-year freeze in non-security discretionary spending included in his FY2011 budget submission to five years.[9] The Obama Administration defines security spending as funding for Department of Defense-Military (subfunction 051); the Department of Energy's National Nuclear Security Administration; International Affairs (function 150, which includes State Department and related agencies); the Department of Homeland Security; and the Department of Veterans Affairs.[10]

Discretionary spending, as noted above, is provided and controlled through appropriations acts, which fund many of the activities commonly associated with such federal government functions as running executive branch agencies, congressional offices and agencies, and international operations of the government. Discretionary spending generally funds program administration costs for entitlement programs such as Social Security, while mandatory spending generally funds Social Security benefits. Thus, the figures showing trends in discretionary budget authority presented below do not reflect the much larger expenditures on program benefits supported by mandatory spending. For some departments, such as Veterans Affairs and Transportation, the division of expenditures into discretionary and mandatory categories can be complex.

Trends in funding of health subfunctions are shown in two separate figures. Larger programs (health care services/subfunction 551 and Medicare/function 570/subfunction 571) are shown in Figure 3, and smaller programs (health research and training/subfunction 552 and consumer and occupational health and safety/subfunction 554) are shown in Figure 4. Veterans' health programs, which fall under the veterans benefits and services function, are also shown in Figure 4 to make comparisons among those programs easier.

Historical Spending Trends

Federal spending trends in functional areas are affected by changing assessments of national priorities, evolving international challenges, economic conditions, as well as changing social characteristics and demographics of the U.S. population.

Some of the trends and events that have had dramatic effects on federal spending are outlined below. Other CRS products provide background on more specific policy areas.

Cold War, Peace Dividend and the Global War on Terror

Trends in Figure 1 reflect shifting national security challenges as well as evolving policy decisions regarding the balance between domestic and defense priorities.

Relations between the United States and its allies on one hand, and the Union of Soviet Socialist Republics (USSR) and its allies on the other was the dominant security concern in the half century following the Second World War. In the early 1970s, U.S. involvement in the Vietnam War wound down, while the United States and the USSR moved towards detente, permitting a thaw in cold war relations between the two superpowers and a reduction in defense spending relative to the size of the economy.[11]

Following intervention by the USSR in Afghanistan in 1979, military spending increased sharply.[12] Defense spending continued to increase until 1986, as concern shifted to domestic priorities and the need to reduce large budget deficits. The collapse in 1989 of most of the Warsaw Pact governments in central and eastern Europe and the 1990-1991 disintegration of the Soviet Union was followed by a reduction in federal defense spending, allowing a "peace dividend" that relaxed fiscal pressures.[13]

Source: CRS, based on OMB data from the FY2012 Budget submission.

Notes: FY2011 are annualized levels from P.L. 111-242; FY2012-FY2016 levels projected. See OMB budget documents for further caveats.

Figure 1. National Defense (050) Subfunctions.

The attacks on the World Trade Center towers in New York City and on the Pentagon on September 11, 2001, were followed by sharp increases in homeland security spending. Defense spending also increased dramatically with the start of the Afghanistan war in October 2001 and the Iraq war in March 2003.[14] While U.S. commitments in Iraq appear to be winding down, the demands of returning troops on Department of Veterans Affairs facilities have grown dramatically.

The Recovery Act

After the financial crisis of 2007-2008 plunged the United States in the deepest economic recession in decades, Congress passed the American Recovery and Reinvestment Act of 2009 (ARRA; P.L. 111-5), often known as the Recovery Act. ARRA includes support for state and local governments in the form of increased infrastructure, Medicaid, school funding, funding for health care IT, extended unemployment benefits, as well as tax cuts and rebates among other provisions.[15] According to initial CBO estimates, ARRA provisions were expected to total $787.2 billion in increased spending and reduced taxes over the FY2009-FY2019 period or just over 5% of GDP in 2008, while a more recent CBO estimate put the total at $814 billion.[16]

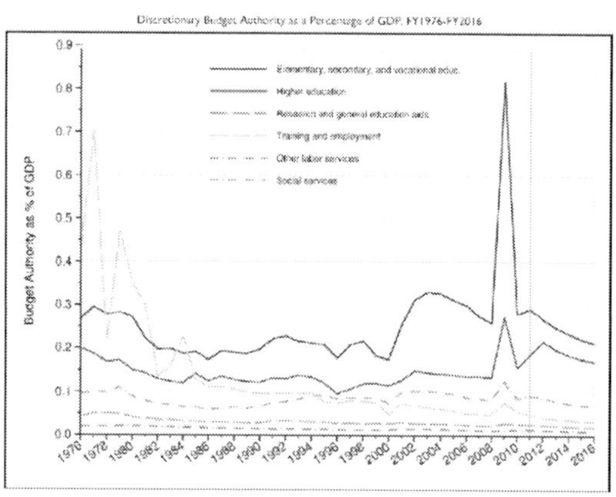

Source: CRS, based on OMB data from the FY2012 Budget submission.

Notes: FY2011 are annualized levels from P.L. 111-242; FY2012-FY2016 levels projected. See OMB budget documents for further caveats.

Figure 2. Education, Training, Employment, and Social Services (500) Subfunctions.

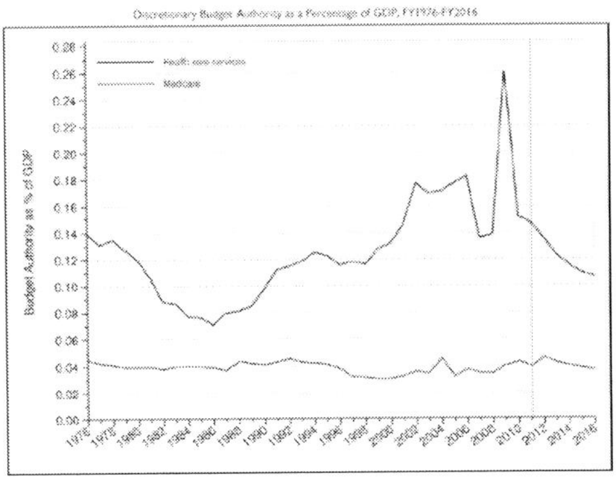

Source: CRS, based on OMB data from the FY2012 Budget submission.

Notes: FY2011 are annualized levels from P.L. 111-242; FY2012-FY2016 levels projected. Discretionary BA for Medicare funds program administration, and does not generally fund program benefits. See OMB budget documents for further caveats.

Figure 3. Health Care Services (Subfunction 551) and Medicare (Subfunction 571).

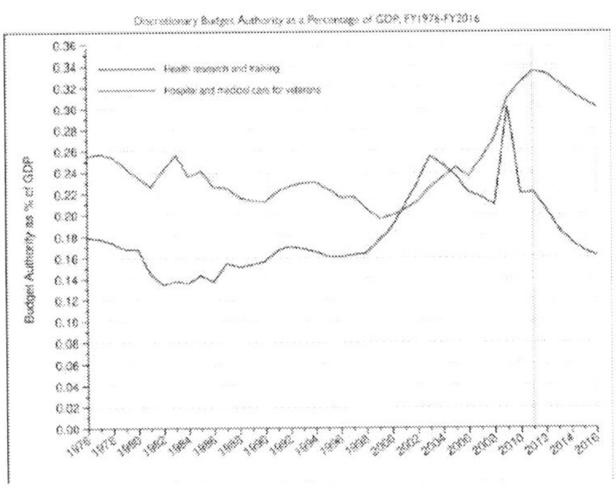

Source: CRS, based on OMB data from the FY2012 Budget submission.

Notes: Hospital and medical care for veterans (703) presented here for comparison, and also appears in **Figure 7**. FY2011 are annualized levels from P.L. 111-242; FY2012-FY2016 levels projected. See OMB budget documents for further caveats.

Figure 4. Smaller Health Subfunctions.

The effects of Recovery Act spending can be seen in **Figure 2**, where pronounced increases in education, training, employment, and social services subfunctions can be seen for FY2009. Smaller increases can be seen in **Figure 8**, which shows energy subfunctions, and in **Figure 9**, which shows natural resources and environment subfunctions.

Source: CRS, based on OMB data from the FY2012 Budget submission.

Notes: Discretionary funding for income security programs supports program administration; most income security benefits are generally funded by mandatory spending, which is not shown here. FY2011 are annualized levels from P.L. 111-242; FY2012-FY2016 levels projected. See OMB budget documents for further caveats.

Figure 5. Income Security (600) Subfunctions.

Source: CRS, based on OMB data from the FY2012 Budget submission.

Notes: Discretionary funding for Social Security supports program administration; Social Security benefits are generally funded by mandatory spending, which is not shown here. FY2011 are annualized levels from P.L. 111-242; FY2012-FY2016 levels projected. See OMB budget documents for further caveats.

Figure 6. Social Security (650) Subfunction.

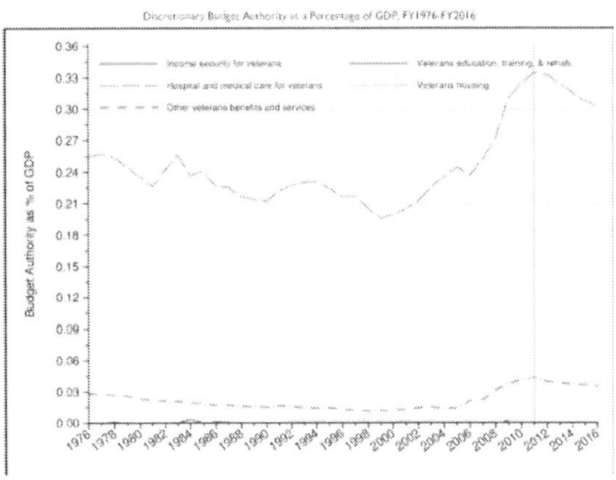

Source: CRS, based on OMB data from the FY2012 Budget submission.

Notes: FY2011 are annualized levels from P.L. 111-242; FY2012-FY2016 levels projected. See OMB budget documents for further caveats. Note that mandatory Veterans Affairs expenditures are not reflected here.

Figure 7. Veterans Benefits and Services (700) Subfunctions.

Negative Budget Authority

Within the federal budget concepts, certain inflows such as offsetting receipts, offsetting collections, some user fees, and "profits" from federal loan programs, are treated as negative budget authority.[17] The federal government uses a modified form of accrual accounting for loan and loan guarantee programs since passage of the Federal Credit Reform Act (FCRA) as well as for certain federal retirement programs.[18] OMB calculates net subsidy rates according to FCRA rules for loan and loan guarantee programs. In some cases, FCRA calculations yield negative net subsidy levels, implying that the federal government appears to make a profit on those loans. FCRA subsidy calculations, however, omit risk adjustments.[19] The true economic cost of federal credit guarantees can be substantially underestimated when risk adjustments are omitted.[20] CBO and OMB include risk adjustments in estimates of the costs associated with the TARP as mandated by the Emergency Economic Stabilization Act of 2008 (EESA; P.L. 110-343).[21]

For example, some Federal Housing Administration mortgage programs have been estimated to yield negative net subsidies, as shown in **Figure 10**.

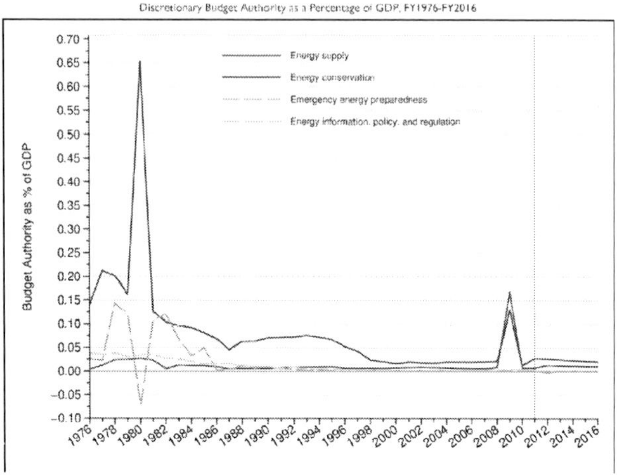

Source: CRS, based on OMB data from the FY2012 Budget submission.

Notes: FY2011 are annualized levels from P.L. 111-242; FY2012-FY2016 levels projected. See OMB budget documents for further caveats.

Figure 8. Energy (270) Subfunctions.

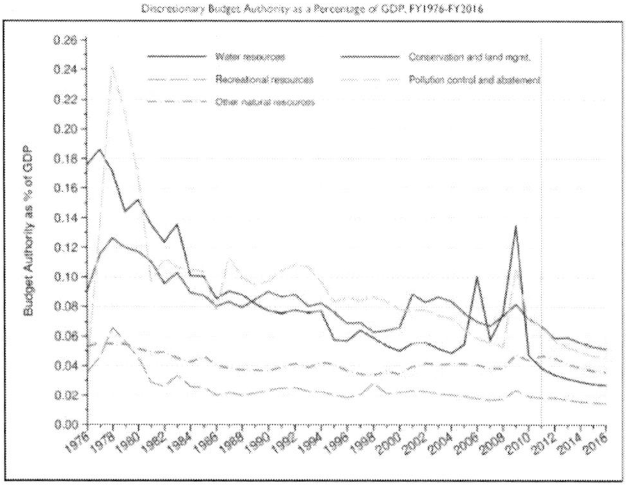

Source: CRS, based on OMB data from the FY2012 Budget submission.

Notes: FY2011 are annualized levels from P.L. 111-242; FY2012-FY2016 levels projected. See OMB budget documents for further caveats.

Figure 9. Natural Resources and Environment (300) Subfunctions.

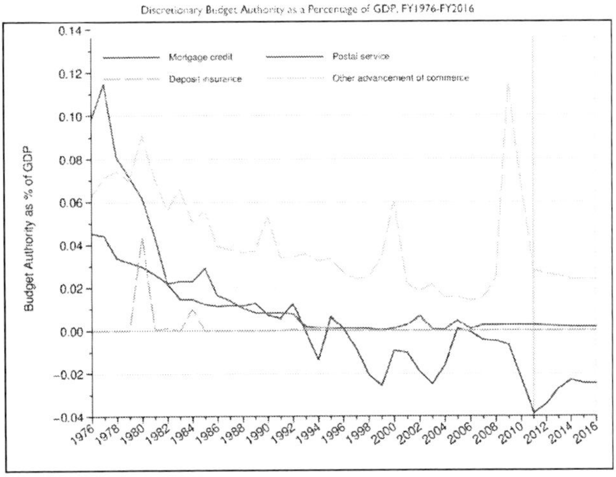

Source: CRS, based on OMB data from FY2012 Budget submission.

Notes: FY2011 are annualized levels from P.L. 111-242; FY2012-FY2016 levels projected. See OMB budget documents for further caveats.

Figure 10. Commerce and Housing Credit Subfunctions.

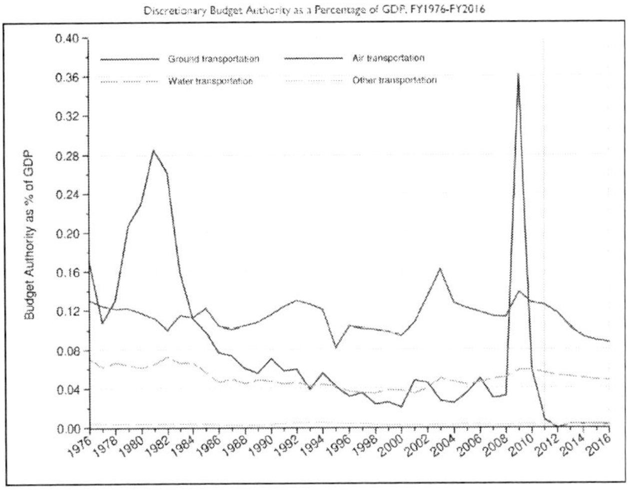

Source: CRS, based on OMB data from FY2012 Budget submission.

Notes: FY2011 are annualized levels from P.L. 111-242; FY2012-FY2016 level projected. See OMB budget documents for further caveats.

Figure 11. Transportation (400) Subfunctions.

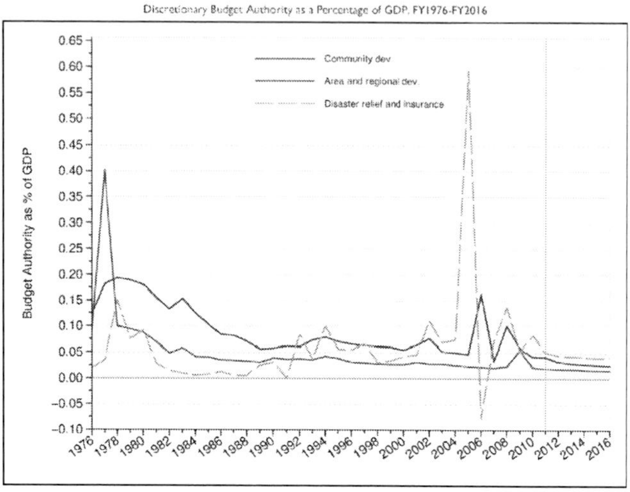

Source: CRS, based on OMB data from FY2012 Budget submission.

Notes: FY2011 are annualized levels from P.L. 111-242; FY2012-FY2016 levels projected. See OMB budget documents for further caveats.

Figure 12. Community and Regional Development (450) Subfunctions.

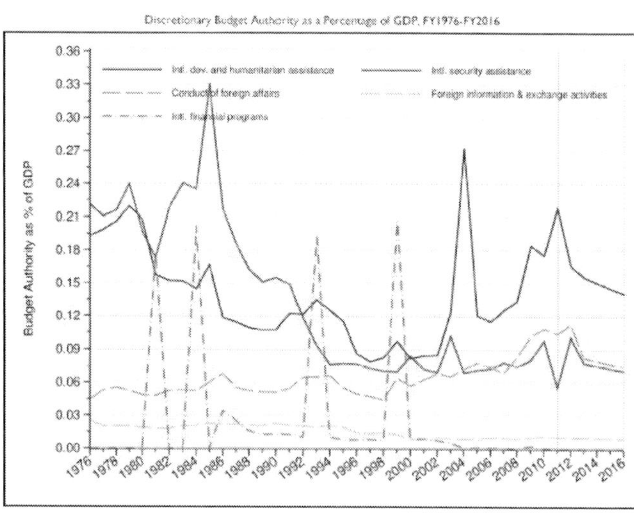

Source: CRS, based on OMB data from the FY2012 Budget submission.

Notes: FY2011 are annualized levels from P.L. 111-242; FY2012-FY2016 levels projected. See OMB budget documents for further caveats.

Figure 13. International Affairs (150) Subfunctions.

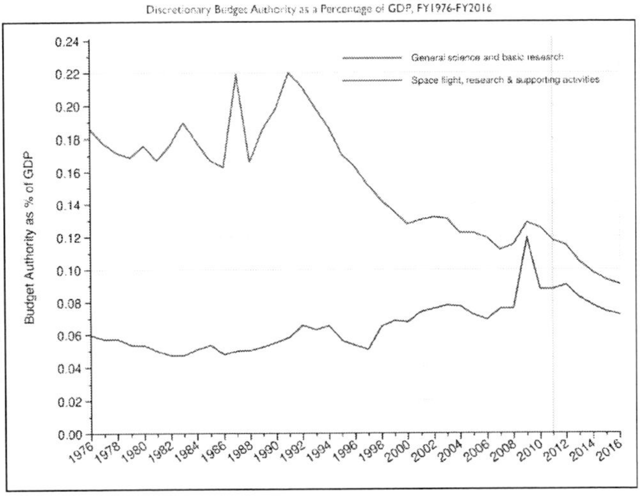

Source: CRS, based on OMB data from the FY2012 Budget submission.

Notes: FY2011 are annualized levels from P.L. 111-242; FY2012-FY2016 levels projected. See OMB budget documents for further caveats.

Figure 14. General Science, Space, and Technology (250) Subfunctions.

Source: CRS, based on OMB data from the FY2012 Budget submission.

Notes: FY2011 are annualized levels from P.L. 111-242; FY2012-FY2016 levels projected. See OMB budget documents for further caveats.

Figure 15. Agriculture (350) Subfunctions.

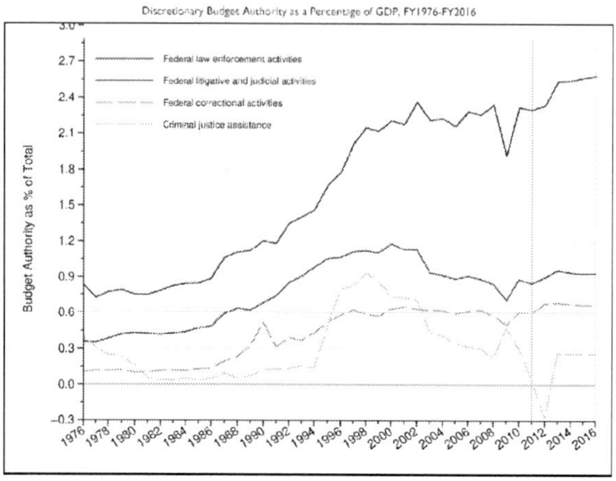

Source: CRS, based on OMB data from the FY2012 Budget submission.

Notes: FY2011 are annualized levels from P.L. 111-242; FY2012-FY2016 levels projected. See OMB budget documents for further caveats.

Figure 16. Administration of Justice (750) Subfunctions.

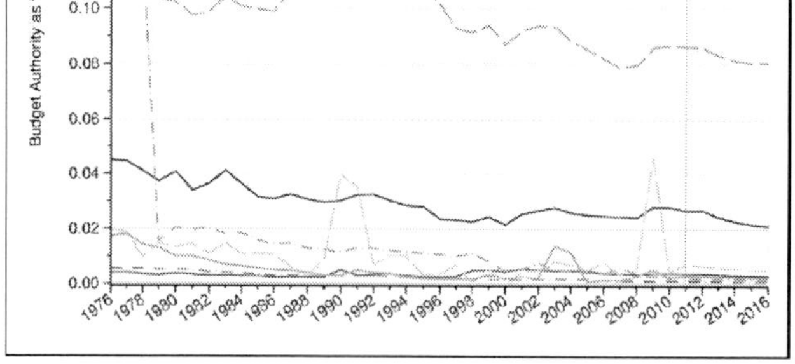

Source: CRS, based on OMB data from the FY2012 Budget submission.

Notes: FY2011 are annualized levels from P.L. 111-242; FY2012-FY2016 levels projected. See OMB budget documents for further caveats.

Figure 17. General Government (800) Subfunctions.

End Notes

[1] The President's FY2012 budget was released on February 14, 2011, and is available at http://www.whitehouse.gov/omb/budget/.
[2] For a broader analysis of discretionary spending, see CRS Report RL34424, *Trends in Discretionary Spending*, by D. Andrew Austin and Mindy R. Levit.
[3] The start of the federal fiscal year was changed from July 1 to October 1 in 1976 to accommodate changes in the congressional budget process. The figures omit data for the Transition Quarter (July 1 to September 30, 1976).
[4] OMB, FY2012 Budget, *Analytic Perspectives* volume, p. 131.
[5] For details, see CRS Report RL30343, *Continuing Resolutions: Latest Action and Brief Overview of Recent Practices*, by Sandy Streeter.
[6] Data in the OMB Public Budget Database reconcile to information presented in the *Historical Tables* volume of the FY2012 budget. The Public Budget Database itself is available here: http://www.whitehouse.gov/omb/budget/Supplemental. For a further description and important caveats, see the *Public Budget Database User Guide*, available at http://www.whitehouse.gov/sites/default/files/omb/budget/fy2012/assets
[7] Table 5.1 of the OMB *Historical Tables* is available at http://www.whitehouse.gov/sites/default/files/omb/budget/fy2012/assets/hist05z1.xls.
[8] For further background on functional categories, see CRS Report 98-280, *Functional Categories of the Federal Budget*, by Bill Heniff Jr.
[9] For details, see CRS Report R41174, *Impact on the Federal Budget of Freezing Non-Security Discretionary Spending*, by Mindy R. Levit.
[10] For a discussion of the definition of security spending, see CRS Report RL34424, *Trends in Discretionary Spending*, by D. Andrew Austin and Mindy R. Levit.
[11] For a history of deficit finance and American wars, see Robert D. Hormats, *The Price of Liberty*, (New York: Times Books, 2007). Also see CRS Report RL3 1176, *Financing Issues and Economic Effects of American Wars*, by Marc Labonte and Mindy R. Levit.
[12] For one view of budgetary politics in the early 1980s, see David Stockman, *The Triumph of Politics*, (New York: Harper & Row, 1986).
[13] The Warsaw Treaty Organization, established in 1955, included Albania, Bulgaria, Czechoslovakia, the German Democratic Republic, Hungary, Poland, Romania, and the Soviet Union.
[14] CRS Report RL33 110, *The Cost of Iraq, Afghanistan, and Other Global War on Terror Operations Since 9/11*, by Amy Belasco.
[15] For more information on the provisions of ARRA, see CRS Report R40537, *American Recovery and Reinvestment Act of 2009 (P.L. 111-5): Summary and Legislative History*, by Clinton T. Brass et al.
[16] For initial estimates, see U.S. Congressional Budget Office, *Cost Estimate For the Conference Agreement For H.R. 1*, February 13, 2009, available at http://cbo.gov/ftpdocs/99xx/doc9989/hr1conference.pdf. For a later assessment, see CBO, Budget and Economic Outlook: An Update, August 2010, Box 1-2, available at http://www.cbo.gov/ftpdocs/117xx/doc1 1705/08-18-Update.pdf.
[17] See OMB, FY2012 Budget, *Analytic Perspectives*, ch. 12, "Budget Concepts." In particular, pp. 122-129 cover these topics.
[18] CRS Report RL30346, *Federal Credit Reform: Implementation of the Changed Budgetary Treatment of Direct Loans and Loan Guarantees*, by James M. Bickley.
[19] While the FCRA calculations include estimates of default costs, they do not discount more volatile income flows, as a private firm would.
[20] U.S. Congressional Budget Office, *Estimating the Value of Subsidies for Federal Loans and Loan Guarantees*, August 2004, available at http://cbo.gov/doc.cfm?index=5751.

[21] U.S. Congressional Budget Office, *The Budget and Economic Outlook: Fiscal Years 2009 to 2019*, January 7, 2009, pp. 25-26, available at http://www.cbo.gov/ftpdocs/99xx/doc9957/01-07-Outlook.pdf; Testimony of Elizabeth Warren, Chair of the Congressional Oversight Panel, in Congress, Senate Banking Committee, *Pulling Back the TARP: Oversight of the Financial Rescue Program*, hearings, 111th Congress, 1st sess., February 5, 2009, available at http://banking

In: Federal Budget Breakdowns ... ISBN: 978-1- 62081-048-4
Editors: S. F. Mathis and I .B. Hewitt

Chapter 2

FY2012 BUDGET HIGHLIGHTS FOR THE HUMAN RESOURCES "SUPERFUNCTION": EDUCATION, TRAINING, SOCIAL SERVICES, HEALTH, INCOME SECURITY, AND VETERANS*

Karen Spar and Gene Falk

SUMMARY

The 112th Congress is focusing attention on short- and long-term efforts to reduce the federal deficit and stabilize the national debt, including proposals to alter the overall size and composition of total federal spending. Components of the federal budget categorized as "human resources" account for the majority of federal outlays (70% in FY2010) and would be affected by these proposals. Six functional categories comprise the human resources "superfunction": education, training, employment, and social services; health (primarily Medicaid); Medicare; income security; Social Security; and veterans benefits and services.

* This is an edited, reformatted and augmented version of the Congressional Research Service Publication, CRS Report for Congress R41827, dated May 17, 2011.

President Obama submitted a detailed FY2012 budget request to Congress on February 14, and in April, he released a set of deficit reduction policies intended to build on the February proposal called the *President's Framework for Shared Prosperity and Shared Fiscal Responsibility.* On April 15, the House passed a concurrent resolution on the FY2012 budget (H.Con.Res. 34) that was based on a document called *Path to Prosperity,* released by Budget Committee Chairman Paul Ryan on April 5. The Senate has not yet acted on a budget resolution for FY2012.

As a share of the national economy, spending for human resources is expected to have peaked at 16.4% of Gross Domestic Product (GDP) in FY2010 and, according to the Congressional Budget Office (CBO), will fall to 14.8% in FY2014. This decline reflects the assumed economic recovery, lower spending for programs that respond automatically to economic conditions (e.g., Unemployment Insurance, Supplemental Nutrition Assistance Program), and expiration of stimulus funding under the American Recovery and Reinvestment Act of 2009 (P.L. 111-5). However, CBO estimates that, with no changes in current law, human resources spending will rise again as a share of GDP and reach 15.7% by FY2021 due to the continuing effects of the baby boom generation's retirement and increased enrollment in Medicare and Social Security, real growth in initial Social Security benefits, medical cost inflation in excess of general inflation, and new spending related to the health care reform law of 2010.

Reflecting these trends, all projected growth in the human resources budget will occur in three functional categories: health (primarily Medicaid), Medicare, and Social Security. CBO estimates that spending for income security will contract as a share of GDP over the next decade, as will spending for the two smallest human resources categories (i.e., education, training, employment, and social services; and veterans benefits and services).

Both the President's budget and H.Con.Res. 34 include provisions intended to reduce spending overall. However, the President's February proposals would result in spending for human resources that would closely follow, and slightly exceed, the CBO current law baseline, while the House resolution sets spending targets that are significantly lower. Specifically, human resources spending would equal 15.9% of GDP in FY2021 under the Administration's February budget and 13.5% under the House resolution, compared to CBO's baseline estimate of 15.7%. The most significant reductions from the CBO baseline, if all provisions assumed in the House resolution were enacted, would occur in three categories: education, training, employment, and social services (the smallest human resources category);

Medicaid; and income security. As widely reported, the House resolution assumes enactment of legislation to convert Medicare into a "premium subsidy" program; however, this change would not occur until FY2022, which is after the resolution's 10-year budget window. Thus, the House resolution sets spending targets for the next 10 years that are relatively close to CBO's baseline projections for Medicare, Social Security, and veterans benefits and services.

INTRODUCTION

Members of Congress and the Obama Administration are engaged in debate over short- and longterm efforts to reduce the federal deficit and stabilize the national debt. Within that debate, attention has focused on proposals to alter the overall size and composition of total federal spending. The bipartisan National Commission on Fiscal Responsibility and Reform issued recommendations for both spending reductions and revenue increases on December 1, 2010.[1] On February 14, 2011, President Obama submitted his detailed FY2012 budget request to Congress, and two months later he released a set of deficit reduction policies intended to build on his February proposal. Unlike the February budget submission, the President's April *Framework for Shared Prosperity and Shared Fiscal Responsibility* does not include detailed proposals and has not been scored by the Congressional Budget Office (CBO).

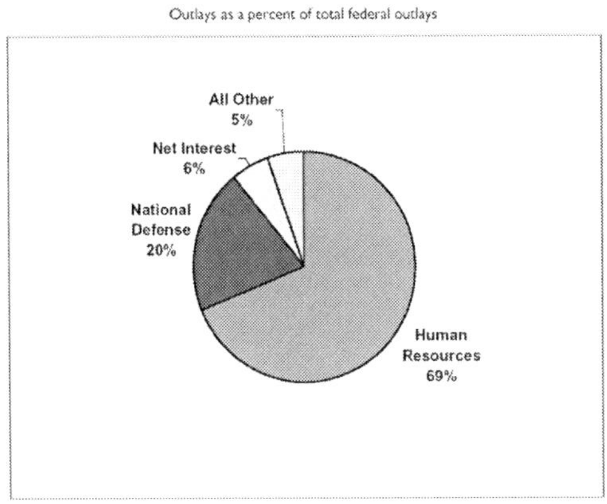

Source: Congressional Research Service (CRS), based on data from the U.S. Office of Management and Budget.

Figure 1. Federal Outlays by Major Budget Category: FY2010.

The House Budget Committee reported a concurrent resolution on the FY2012 budget (H.Con.Res. 34) that was based on a document titled *Path to Prosperity,* released by Budget Committee Chairman Paul Ryan on April 5. The full House passed H.Con.Res. 34 on April 15 after defeating substitute versions offered by the Congressional Black Caucus (H.Amdt. 256), the Congressional Progressive Caucus (H.Amdt. 257), the Republican Study Committee (H.Amdt. 258), and the Democratic Caucus (H.Amdt. 259).[2] The Senate has not yet acted on a budget resolution for FY2012.

This CRS report highlights spending trends and key policy initiatives in the President's February budget and April *Framework*, and in the House-passed budget resolution, for the six functional categories of the federal budget that comprise the human resources "superfunction." The six human resources functions (and their function codes) are

- education, training, employment, and social services (Function 500);
- health (primarily Medicaid) (Function 550);
- Medicare (Function 570);
- income security (Function 600);
- Social Security (Function 650); and
- veterans benefits and services (Function 700).

As shown in **Figure 1**, the human resources superfunction accounts for the majority of federal spending, with nearly 70% of federal outlays in FY2010.

This report does not discuss the broad outlines of the FY2012 budget proposals, such as their projected levels of total spending, revenues, or deficits. Moreover, the report does not attempt to quantify the costs or savings associated with specific proposals. The purpose of the report is to give a very broad overview of the spending trends and policy recommendations proposed by the Administration and the House budget resolution—specifically, for the human resources budget functions—as background for the detailed budget and appropriations discussions that are taking place this year.

What are Budget Functions and Superfunctions?

The federal budget is divided into 20 functional categories (e.g., national defense, health, energy, transportation), which are further divided into subfunctions.[3] These functional categories provide a broad statement of budget priorities and facilitate the analysis of trends in related programs; they are used for informational purposes in the congressional budget process. For purposes of analysis, some budget functions are grouped together into budget "superfunctions" (e.g., national defense, human resources, physical resources).

Congress begins formal consideration of the annual budget resolution after the President submits his detailed budget request for the coming fiscal year. (For example, as noted, President Obama submitted his FY2012 budget to Congress in February and the House passed a budget resolution in April.) The congressional budget resolution is not signed by the President and does not become public law. Rather, it is an internal blueprint for Congress to use in its consideration of legislation and spending for the coming fiscal year. The resolution establishes target levels for spending (budget authority and outlays) and revenues, along with an estimate of the deficit (or surplus) and the national debt. The resolution includes targets for the coming fiscal year and projected levels for subsequent years.

Unlike the President's budget request submitted in February, the congressional budget resolution does not specify spending levels by program but instead establishes aggregate spending targets for each of the functional categories referred to above. These aggregate amounts are based on certain "assumptions" about spending for specific programs, but the assumptions are not typically specified in the resolution, nor are they binding on the appropriations committees or committees with jurisdiction over mandatory spending programs or tax provisions. Key assumptions are sometimes identified in the Budget Committee report that accompanies the concurrent resolution. The congressional budget process allows for several enforcement mechanisms to ensure compliance with overall targets established in the resolution.[4]

Organization of This Report

This report continues with a brief overview of the human resources superfunction as a whole, looking at long-term historical and future projected trends in spending under current law, in comparison with other major components of the federal budget. The section compares human resources spending under current law, as estimated by CBO, with the President's February budget request and amounts included in the House budget resolution.

The next section identifies selected overarching policies included in the Administration and House budgets that are intended to reduce spending and/or stabilize the national debt; these policies could directly or indirectly result in lower spending across budget functions. The remainder of the report focuses on the six individual categories that comprise the human resources superfunction. Each section compares the CBO current law baseline for FY20 11 through FY2021 with the President's February proposal (as re-estimated by CBO) and the House budget resolution, in constant FY2011 dollars. An **Appendix** to the report includes a table showing each of the human resources budget functions as a percentage of GDP, and two tables showing federal budget authority and outlays (in nominal dollars) for each of the six functions.

Sources of information used in this report include the following:

- The Obama Administration's FY2012 budget documents: http://www.whitehouse.gov/omb/budget.
- White House fact sheet on *The President's Framework for Shared Prosperity and Shared Fiscal Responsibility*: http://www.whitehouse.gov/the-press-office/2011/04/13/fact-sheet-presidents-framework-shared-prosperity-and-shared-fiscal-resp.
- *An Analysis of the President's Budgetary Proposals for Fiscal Year 2012*, by the Congressional Budget Office: http://www.cbo.gov/doc.cfm?index=12130.
- *The Path to Prosperity: Restoring America's Promise*, House Budget Committee: http://budget.house.gov/UploadedFiles/PathToProsperity FY2012.pdf.
- H.Con.Res. 34, as passed by the House, and the accompanying House Budget Committee report (H.Rept. 112-58).
- *Long-Term Analysis of a Budget Proposal by Chairman Ryan*, by the Congressional Budget Office: http://www.cbo.gov/doc.cfm?index=12128.

THE HUMAN RESOURCES SUPERFUNCTION

Current Law

Figure 2 shows the trend in federal outlays for major categories of the federal budget, as a share of the national economy, from FY1962 through FY2010. The figure also shows CBO's projections for these categories, assuming no change in current law, through FY2021. The figure illustrates the growth in spending for human resources over the last five decades, and shows the importance of this component of the budget, in relation to other government spending. Specifically, the figure shows that outlays for human resources, as a percentage of Gross Domestic Product (GDP), have grown substantially since 1962, when they accounted for 5.6% of GDP. CBO expects they will have peaked in FY2010, at 16.4%, and will fall to 14.8% in FY2014. This pattern reflects the assumed economic recovery, lower spending for programs that respond automatically to economic conditions such as Unemployment Insurance and the Supplemental Nutrition Assistance Program (SNAP),[5] and the expiration of all stimulus funding.[6]

Beginning in FY2015, however, human resources spending would rise again as a share of GDP, according to CBO, reaching 15.7% by FY2021. While this is lower than the FY2010 level of 16.4% of GDP, it still exceeds the pre-recession (2007) level of 12.7%. Fueling this increased spending are several factors, including the continuing effects of the baby boom generation's retirement and increased enrollment in Medicare and Social Security, certain program design features such as wage indexing in Social Security (which allows initial monthly benefits to replace a constant proportion of pre-retirement earnings and keep pace with rising living standards), medical cost inflation in excess of general inflation, and new spending attributable to implementation of the health care reform law of 2010.[7]

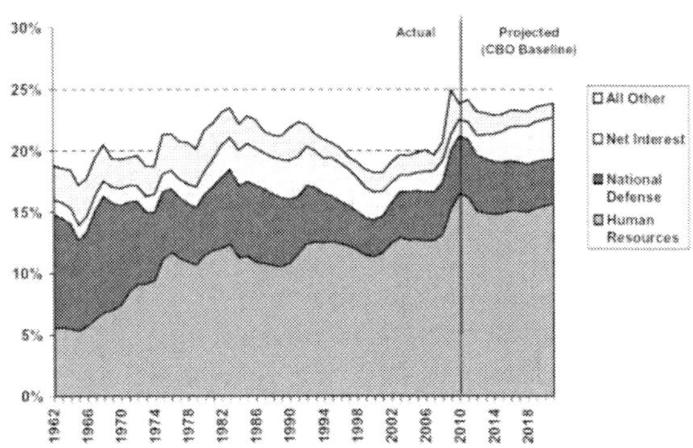

Source: Congressional Research Service (CRS), based on data from the U.S. Office of Management and Budget (OMB) and the Congressional Budget Office (CBO).

Notes: GDP for FY2011 through FY2021 is based on CBO's forecasts and projections. Outlays in FY2011 were estimated prior to enactment of the full-year continuing appropriations resolution, P.L. 112-10.

Figure 2. Federal Outlays by Major Budget Category as Percent of GDP: FY1962-FY2021.

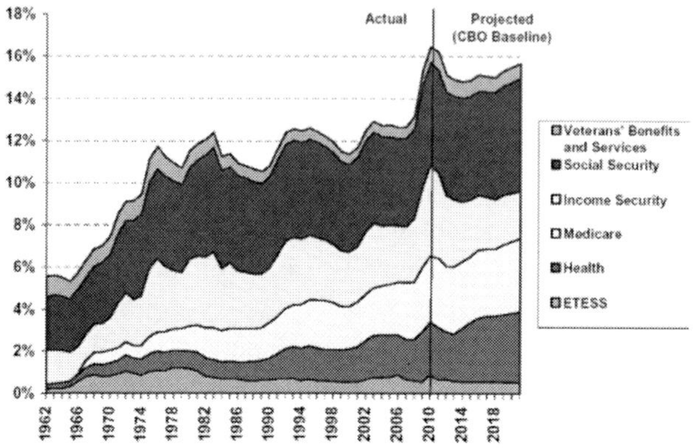

Source: Congressional Research Service (CRS), based on data from the U.S. Office of Management and Budget (OMB) and the Congressional Budget Office (CBO).

Notes: GDP for FY2011 through FY2021 is based on CBO's forecasts and projections. Outlays in FY2011 were estimated prior to enactment of the full-year continuing appropriations resolution, P.L. 112-10. ETESS = Education, Training, Employment, and Social Services.

Figure 3. Federal Outlays for Human Resources Budget Functions as Percent of GDP: FY1962 through FY2021.

The effect of these factors can be seen in **Figure 3**, which shows the trend in outlays for each of the six human resources budget functions, as a share of GDP, from FY1962 through FY2010 and then projected through FY2021. The figure illustrates that spending in the human resources superfunction has been increasingly dominated by four categories: health (Function 500, which primarily consists of Medicaid), Medicare (Function 570), income security (Function 600), and Social Security (Function 650). With no change in current law, CBO projects that spending for income security as a share of GDP will contract over the next decade, as will spending for the two smallest functions—education, training, employment, and social services (Function 500), and veterans benefits and services (Function 700). On the other hand, CBO projects that spending for three functions—health (mostly Medicaid), Medicare, and Social Security—will increasingly consume more of the economy as the population ages and the cost of health care continues to rise.[8]

Most federal low-income programs are included in one of the human resources budget functions, most likely Function 500 (education, training, employment, and social services) or Function 600 (income security), in addition to Function 550, which includes Medicaid and the State Children's

Health Insurance Program (CHIP).[9] A review of these programs shows the same trend discussed above; that is, health care is growing as a share of the economy while spending for other services (other than Social Security) contracts. A CRS analysis of federal outlays for major federal low- income programs shows aggregate spending for these programs, as a share of GDP, will have peaked in FY2010 but will rise again starting in FY2013. However, all projected growth in spending for these low-income programs will be for health programs (specifically Medicaid, CHIP, and the refundable portion of a health insurance tax credit created under the 2010 health care reform law, which is scheduled to begin in 2014). With no change in current law, spending for non-health low-income programs will increasingly diminish as a share of the economy over the next decade.[10]

Pending Proposals

Figure 4 compares total estimated outlays for the human resources superfunction, as a share of GDP, under CBO's baseline, President Obama's February request, and the House budget resolution, from FY2011 through FY2021. The figure shows that the President's budget closely follows and slightly exceeds the CBO baseline, while the House budget resolution would result in significantly lower spending as a share of the national economy. All three budgets project an immediate drop in spending. Under the CBO baseline and Administration budget, spending would then be relatively flat for most of the period before gradually increasing in the final years of the decade. Under the House budget resolution, spending would continue a gradual decline throughout most of the period, but would also rise slightly at the end of the decade. As stated earlier, CBO projects that human resources spending will equal 15.7% of GDP in FY2021 with no change in policy. This compares with 15.9% under the Administration's budget and 13.5% under the House resolution.

Later sections of this report discuss each of the human resources functional categories specifically, and show trends in projected outlays under the CBO baseline, the President's February request, and the House resolution. As discussed above, CBO expects continued growth in the two health-related functions as well as Social Security. While the House budget resolution assumes dramatically lower spending for the health function that includes Medicaid, it would result in no significant changes in spending for Medicare or Social Security over the next 10 years. Instead, H.Con.Res. 34 sets targets that would lower spending from the current law baseline in two additional functions: education, training, employment, and social services, and income security.

OVERARCHING POLICY PROPOSALS

As noted in the beginning of this report, policymakers are concerned about the current and projected future size of the federal deficit, or the gap between spending and revenues.[11] Both the Administration and House budget proposals include overarching policies intended to constrain growth in federal spending, among other deficit-reduction proposals. These policies, summarized below, would affect spending in most of the functional categories that are the focus of this report.

Administration Budget

- In its February budget submission, the Administration proposed to freeze non-security discretionary spending through FY2015 at FY2010 levels.[12] This would not be an across-the-board reduction (affecting all programs equally) but rather an overall freeze with critical areas singled out for increased spending. Specific amounts are identified in the Administration's budget documents.
- In his April *Framework*, President Obama proposed additional reductions in non- security discretionary spending, beyond those included in the February budget. According to a White House fact sheet, these reductions would be consistent with the spending recommendations of the National Commission on Fiscal Responsibility and Reform over the next decade. [13]
- Also in the April *Framework*, President Obama announced a "debt failsafe" that would trigger further reductions in spending (including mandatory spending and tax expenditures). This provision would establish that if, by 2014, the projected ratio of debt to GDP is not stabilized and shown to be declining during the second half of the decade, automatic across-the-board spending cuts would be triggered. The White House fact sheet notes that this trigger would not apply to Social Security, low-income programs,[14] or benefits for Medicare enrollees.

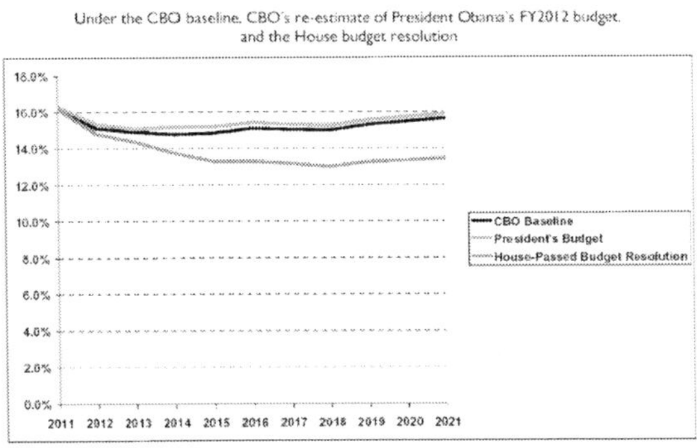

Source: Congressional Research Service (CRS), based on data from the Congressional Budget Office (CBO) and the House Budget Committee (HBC).

Notes: GDP for FY2011 through FY2021 is based on CBO's forecasts and projections. Outlays in FY2011 were estimated prior to enactment of the full-year continuing appropriations resolution, P.L. 112-10.

Figure 4. Federal Outlays for Human Resources Budget Functions as Percent of GDP: FY2011 through FY2021.

House Budget Resolution

- The House budget resolution establishes spending targets that assume a reduction in discretionary non-security spending to below FY2008 levels and a five-year freeze.[15] As noted earlier, the congressional budget resolution does not establish spending levels for individual programs; these decisions are made through the appropriations process, within the overall spending targets set by the budget resolution.[16]
- The House budget resolution also calls for a series of steps intended to enforce both the discretionary spending and the total spending caps included in the resolution. These mechanisms would trigger automatic across-the-board spending reductions unless Congress moves to avoid such across-the-board reductions through enactment of legislation under expedited procedures. Social Security would be exempt from these enforcement mechanisms.

These overarching proposals are key components of both the Administration and House budget plans. They are reflected in the trend lines shown above in **Figure 4** and in the following sections, which illustrate and discuss the trends in projected outlays for each of the six functions categorized as human resources.

FUNCTION 500: EDUCATION, TRAINING, EMPLOYMENT AND SOCIAL SERVICES (ETESS)

Function 500 includes funding for the Department of Education (ED), social services programs within the Department of Health and Human Services (HHS), and employment and training programs within the Department of Labor (DOL). It also contains funding for the Library of Congress and independent research and art agencies such as the Corporation for Public Broadcasting, the Smithsonian Institution, the National Gallery of Art, the John F. Kennedy Center for the Performing Arts, the National Endowment for the Arts, and the National Endowment for the Humanities.[17] Most spending under Function 500 is discretionary. However, mandatory spending includes student financial assistance, some training and employment services, and Social Services Block Grants.

Spending under this function is divided among the following six subfunctions:[18]

- elementary, secondary, and vocational education;
- higher education;
- research and general education aids;
- training and employment;
- other labor services; and
- social services.

Figure 5 shows estimated outlays for Function 500 programs, from FY2011 through FY2021 in constant FY2011 dollars, under the CBO baseline, the Administration's February budget request, and the House budget resolution. As illustrated, the Administration's February request exceeds the CBO baseline for most of the period by a relatively small and gradually diminishing amount, while the House resolution envisions spending at substantially lower levels than the CBO baseline. By FY2021, Function 500 spending under the Administration's February budget would be virtually identical to the CBO baseline (1% higher), while the House budget resolution assumes spending would be 36% below the baseline. (Note that the President's April *Framework* proposes additional reductions in discretionary spending that presumably would lower estimated spending under the Administration's budget for Function 500.)

As a function dominated by discretionary spending, Function 500 would be affected by the Administration's proposals to reduce and freeze overall discretionary non-security spending through FY2015; however, Function 500 also includes several policy areas identified by the White House as critical investments for the future. These include education and workforce development, where the Administration has proposed a variety of reforms and program consolidations, as well as increased spending for certain programs, offset by termination of others. Certain savings would be achieved from changes to Pell grants and student loans, which would help offset the cost of maintaining the current maximum Pell grant award.[19] The Administration also proposes to permanently extend and index the American Opportunity Credit, a partially refundable tax credit for the costs of higher education that was originally created by the American Recovery and Reinvestment Act of 2009 (ARRA, P.L. 111-5).

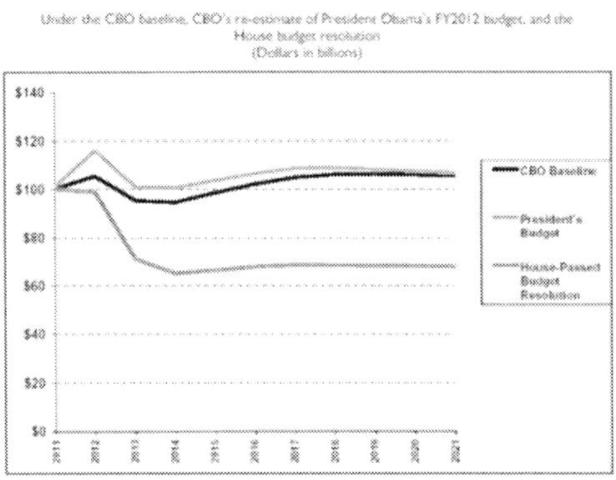

Source: Congressional Research Service (CRS), based on data from the Congressional Budget Office (CBO) and the House Budget Committee (HBC).

Notes: Inflation adjustment is based on the implicit price deflator for the Gross Domestic Product (GDP) based on CBO's forecast and projections. Outlays in FY2011 were estimated prior to enactment of the full-year continuing appropriations resolution, P.L. 112-10. ETESS = Education, Training, Employment, and Social Services.

Figure 5. Federal Outlays for the ETESS Budget Function, in Constant FY2011 Dollars: FY2011 through FY2021.

As displayed in **Figure 5**, spending for Function 500 under the House budget resolution would drop sharply in FY2013 and stay relatively constant for the rest of the decade. This trend reflects the deeper overall discretionary spending cuts and freeze assumed by the House resolution, including consolidation and termination of various job training, elementary and secondary education, and cultural programs. The House resolution also assumes certain changes to Pell grants and student loans, but would adopt a "sustainable" maximum Pell grant award rather than the current maximum level.

FUNCTION 550: HEALTH

Function 550 includes most direct health care services programs, most notably Medicaid. Other health programs in this function fund anti-bioterrorism activities, national biomedical research, activities to protect the health of the general population and workers in their places of employment, health services for under-served populations, and training for the health care workforce. Some of the HHS agencies funded in this function include the National Institutes of Health, Centers for Disease Control and Prevention, Health Resources and Services Administration, and the Food and Drug Administration. The major mandatory programs in this function are Medicaid, the State Children's Health Insurance Program (CHIP), federal and retirees' health benefits, and health care for Medicare-eligible military retirees.

Spending under this function is divided among the following three subfunctions:[20]

- health care services,
- health research and training, and
- consumer and occupational health and safety.

Figure 6 shows estimated outlays for Function 550 programs, from FY2011 through FY2021 in constant FY2011 dollars, under the CBO baseline, the Administration's February budget request, and the House budget resolution. The difference in trends is stark. The Administration budget would track closely with CBO, which expects an initial drop in Medicaid spending in FY2012, due to the scheduled expiration of enhanced federal matching to states initially authorized by ARRA, and the effects of the economic recovery on the Medicaid caseload. However, spending would then climb sharply, starting in FY2013, under both the CBO baseline and the Administration's February budget. The House budget resolution, on the other hand, envisions a decrease in spending until FY2014, followed by a relatively flat line through FY2018, and a slight increase for the balance of the decade. In FY2021, the Administration's February budget would result in estimated outlays only slightly (2%) lower than the CBO baseline, while outlays would be 50% lower under the House budget resolution's spending targets.

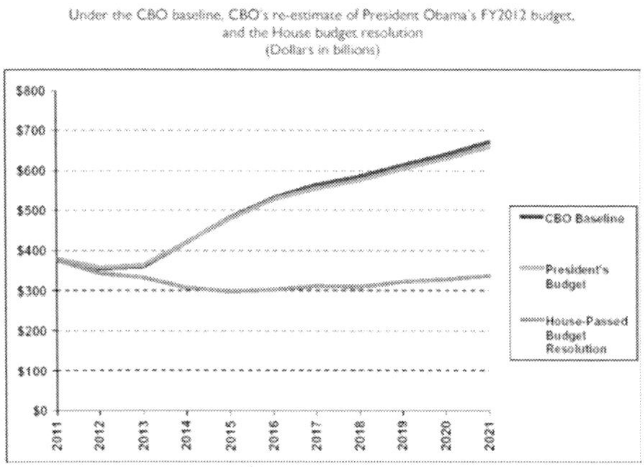

Source: Congressional Research Service (CRS), based on data from the Congressional Budget Office (CBO) and the House Budget Committee (HBC).

Notes: Inflation adjustment is based on the implicit price deflator for the Gross Domestic Product (GDP) based on CBO's forecast and projections. Outlays in FY2011 were estimated prior to enactment of the full-year continuing appropriations resolution, P.L. 112-10.

Figure 6. Federal Outlays for the Health Budget Function, in Constant 2011 Dollars: FY2011 through FY2021.

Medicaid is the primary driver of spending in Function 550. In its request for Medicaid and Medicare (discussed below), the Administration cites the major changes to both programs already enacted in the Patient Protection and Affordable Care Act of 2010 (PPACA, P.L. 111-148, as amended by P.L. 111-152). The Administration's FY2012 budget includes additional Medicaid proposals intended to improve program integrity (reduce fraud, waste, and abuse), limit reimbursement rates for durable medical equipment, simplify the federal-state matching formulas under Medicaid and CHIP,[21] and improve patient safety. The President's *Framework* also expresses support for proposals to reform service delivery to high-cost beneficiaries, including those eligible for both Medicaid and Medicare (dual eligibles), and calls on the National Governors Association to make additional recommendations for Medicaid reform.

The House Budget Committee, in its accompanying report, notes that the budget resolution assumes a "fundamental reform" of Medicaid. The report lists a series of "potential approaches," including conversion of the federal share of Medicaid spending into an allotment (a block grant), which would be indexed for inflation and population growth. The committee advocates repealing the Medicaid expansions enacted in PPACA, which are scheduled to begin in 2014, and the PPACA provisions authorizing subsidies to help low-income individuals purchase health insurance through exchanges. The resolution also assumes elimination of the individual mandate to purchase insurance, established under PPACA. The House budget resolution further assumes savings would be achieved by repealing any unspent funds provided under ARRA and other associated provisions in PPACA.[22]

FUNCTION 570: MEDICARE

Function 570 includes only the Medicare program, which provides health insurance to individuals age 65 or older and certain persons with disabilities. Nearly 99% of spending in this function is mandatory, and almost all of the mandatory spending consists of payments for Medicare benefits. Congress provides an annual appropriation for the costs of administering and monitoring the Medicare program.[23]

Figure 7 shows estimated outlays for Medicare, from FY2011 through FY2021 in constant FY2011 dollars, under the CBO baseline, the Administration's February budget request, and the House budget resolution. The figure illustrates relatively little difference between the three, which all show significantly increasing spending for Medicare throughout the decade, caused by an aging population and rising health care costs. Estimated spending in FY2021 would exceed the CBO current law baseline by 5% under the President's February budget and would be 3% lower than CBO's projections under the House resolution.

As noted above, the Administration's budget cites changes to Medicare already enacted in PPACA, and includes various proposals intended to build on these provisions. In addition, the February budget proposed a 10-year freeze on physician payment rates under Medicare at FY2011 levels (the so-called "doc fix"), which would otherwise decline under the sustainable growth rate formula in current law.[24] The increased cost of this proposal would be offset by specified savings during the first two years. The April *Framework* assumes, but does not specify, additional aggregate savings that would fully pay for the "doc fix" provision over the 10-year budget window. The *Framework* says the Independent Payment Advisory Board (IPAB), created by PPACA, will set a lower target of Medicare growth per beneficiary and be given additional tools to promote quality care and reduce costs.[25] The Administration's budget also includes proposals to cut prescription drug costs, and reduce Medicare waste, fraud, and abuse.

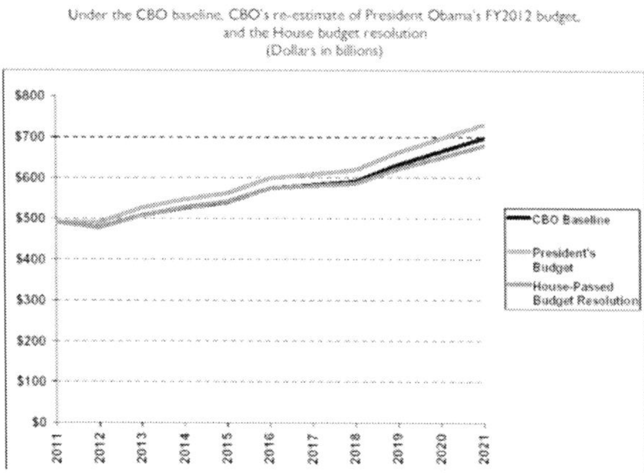

Source: Congressional Research Service (CRS), based on data from the Congressional Budget Office (CBO) and the House Budget Committee (HBC).

Notes: Inflation adjustment is based on the implicit price deflator for the Gross Domestic Product (GDP) based on CBO's forecast and projections. Outlays in FY2011 were estimated prior to enactment of the full-year continuing appropriations resolution, P.L. 112-10.

Figure 7. Federal Outlays for the Medicare Budget Function, in Constant FY2011 Dollars: FY2011 through FY2021.

One of the most widely reported provisions in the House budget resolution assumes enactment of legislation to convert Medicare into a "premium subsidy" program. However, as envisioned in the budget resolution, this change would not take effect until FY2022, which is beyond the resolution's 10-year budget window and is therefore not reflected in **Figure 7**. The resolution assumes additional changes affecting Medicare, including enactment of a long-term solution to the physician payment rate formula. The resolution contains a "reserve fund" to accommodate the SGR fix; this provision would allow for consideration of legislation that would reform SGR, as long as the legislation did not increase the deficit for the period FY2012-FY2021. The resolution also assumes a requirement that any potential savings in Medicare be reinvested into the program; elimination of the IPAB; and enactment of changes to laws governing medical liability, including limits on noneconomic and punitive damages.[26]

FUNCTION 600: INCOME SECURITY

Function 600 includes a range of income security programs that provide cash or near-cash assistance (e.g., housing, nutrition, and energy assistance) to low-income persons, and benefits to certain retirees, persons with disabilities, and the unemployed. Housing assistance programs account for the largest share of discretionary funding in this function. Major federal entitlement programs in this function include Unemployment Insurance, Trade Adjustment Assistance income support, the Supplemental Nutrition Assistance Program

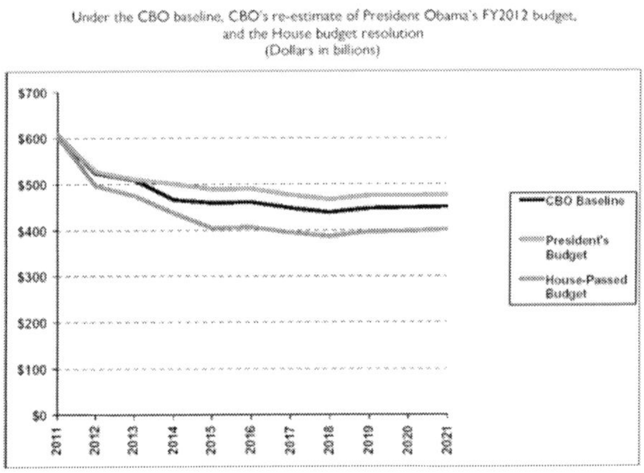

Source: Congressional Research Service (CRS), based on data from the Congressional Budget Office (CBO) and the House Budget Committee (HBC).

Notes: : Inflation adjustment is based on the implicit price deflator for the Gross Domestic Product (GDP) based on CBO's forecast and projections. Outlays in FY2011 were estimated prior to enactment of the full-year continuing appropriations resolution, P.L. 112-10.

Figure 8. Federal Outlays for the Income Security Budget Function, in Constant FY2011 Dollars: FY2011 through FY2021.

(SNAP, formerly food stamps), Temporary Assistance for Needy Families (TANF), foster care, and Supplemental Security Income (SSI). The refundable portion of the Earned Income Tax Credit (EITC) and the refundable Additional Child Tax Credit (ACTC)[27] are also included in this function. Federal and other retirement and disability programs comprise approximately one-third of funds in Function 600.

Spending under this function is divided among the following six subfunctions:[28]

- general retirement and disability insurance (excluding Social Security),
- federal employee retirement and disability,
- unemployment compensation,
- housing assistance,
- food and nutrition assistance, and
- other income security.

Figure 8 shows estimated outlays for Function 600 programs, from FY2011 through FY2021 in constant FY2011 dollars, under the CBO baseline, the Administration's February budget request, and the House budget resolution. The figure shows the Administration's budget is identical to the CBO baseline until FY2013. Both lines then show decreased spending through FY2018, but outlays would decline at a slower rate under the Administration's February proposals. The CBO baseline assumes recession-related spending will decline, and also assumes expiration of certain temporary provisions, including expansions of the EITC, ACTC, and extended Unemployment Insurance. The House budget resolution shows a sharper drop in spending continuing through FY2015, with outlays leveling off and staying relatively constant through FY2021. The President's budget projects FY2021 outlays would be 6% higher than the CBO baseline, while they would be 11% lower than CBO under the House budget resolution.

Like the CBO baseline, the Administration's budget assumes reduced recession-related spending for UI and SNAP as the economy recovers. The Administration's proposals to reduce discretionary spending also would apply to certain programs in this function, and include a relatively deep cut in the Low-Income Home Energy Assistance Program (LIHEAP). However, the Administration also proposes to permanently extend certain tax provisions, including expansions of the EITC and the ACTC, which were initially authorized under ARRA and are scheduled to expire under current law. The

President's budget includes provisions intended to address the unfunded liabilities in the UI system and the Pension Benefit Guaranty Corporation.

As shown in the figure, the House budget resolution assumes lower spending for Function 600 programs, at least partially due to deeper cuts in discretionary non-security spending. In its accompanying report, the House Budget Committee also cites conversion of SNAP (food stamps) into a block grant to states as a possible policy option in this category, with state allotments indexed for food inflation and eligibility, starting in FY2015. The report also refers to a welfare reform provision that is discussed more fully in Chairman Ryan's *Path to Prosperity*. The 1996 welfare reform law applied work requirements and time limits to recipients of cash aid under TANF; such requirements would also be applied to recipients of SNAP benefits and housing assistance, according to Chairman Ryan's description of the budget resolution. The resolution assumes enactment of a provision that would require federal employees to contribute a greater share toward their retirement; elimination of the Home Affordable Modification Program (HAMP), which was intended to help homeowners avoid foreclosure; and reform of the PBGC.

FUNCTION 650: SOCIAL SECURITY

Function 650 consists of the payroll tax-financed programs that are collectively known as Social Security: Old-Age and Survivors Insurance and Disability Insurance (OASDI). This function includes both Social Security benefit payments (mandatory) and funds to administer the program (discretionary).[29]

Figure 9 shows estimated outlays for Function 650, from FY2011 through FY2021 in constant FY2011 dollars, under the CBO baseline, the Administration's February budget request, and the House budget resolution. The figure shows virtually no difference between the three lines, as neither the Administration nor the House budget resolution assumes significant policy changes in Social Security within the 10-year budget window. Note that **Figure 9** shows outlays for both the on-budget and off-budget portions of Social Security.[30]

Although the Administration's budget contains no specific Social Security proposals, President Obama expressed support for bipartisan efforts to strengthen Social Security for the long term and put forth a set of principles to govern these reform efforts.[31] These principles were reiterated in the April *Framework* and include strengthening retirement security for low-income and vulnerable beneficiaries and maintaining "robust" disability and survivors' benefits; no "privatization" of Social Security; restoration of long-term solvency; and no reduction in basic benefits for current beneficiaries or "slashing" of benefits for future generations.

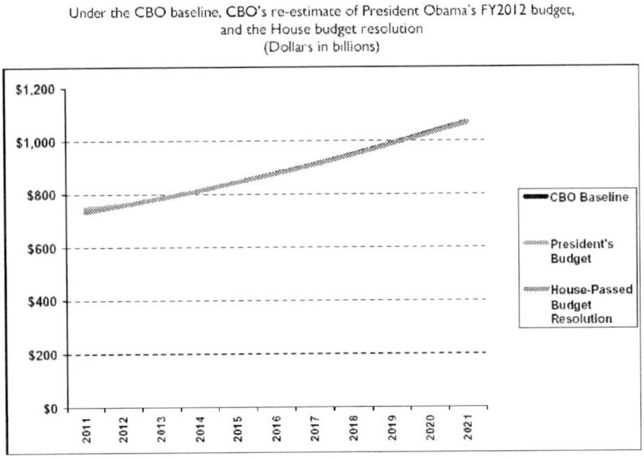

Source: Congressional Research Service (CRS), based on data from the Congressional Budget Office (CBO) and the House Budget Committee (HBC).

Notes: Inflation adjustment is based on the implicit price deflator for the Gross Domestic Product (GDP) based on CBO's forecast and projections. Outlays in FY2011 were estimated prior to enactment of the full-year continuing appropriations resolution, P.L. 112-10.

Figure 9. Federal Outlays for the Social Security Budget Function, in Constant FY2011 Dollars: FY2011 through FY2021.

In its report on the budget resolution, the House Budget Committee refers to the December 2010 recommendations of the President's Commission on Fiscal Responsibility and Reform as demonstration "that there is a bipartisan way forward" on Social Security reform. In the interim, the resolution would require the Social Security Board of Trustees to recommend statutory reforms to the President in any year when the Trustees find the 75-year actuarial balance and the annual balance in the 75th year are in deficit. The President would be required to submit legislation to implement these recommendations by a certain deadline and congressional committees would be required to report legislation under expedited procedures.

Function 700: Veterans Benefits and Services

Function 700 covers the programs of the Department of Veterans Affairs (VA), including veterans' medical care, compensation and pensions, education and rehabilitation benefits, and housing programs. It also includes the Department of Labor's Veterans' Employment and Training Service, the United States Court of Appeals for Veterans Claims, and the American Battle Monuments Commission. This function includes both mandatory and discretionary spending accounts. Mandatory funding supports disability compensation, pension benefits, education, vocational rehabilitation, life insurance, and burial benefits, among other benefits and services. Discretionary funding supports a broad array of benefits and services; almost 90% of appropriated funding in Function 700 goes to veterans' health care.

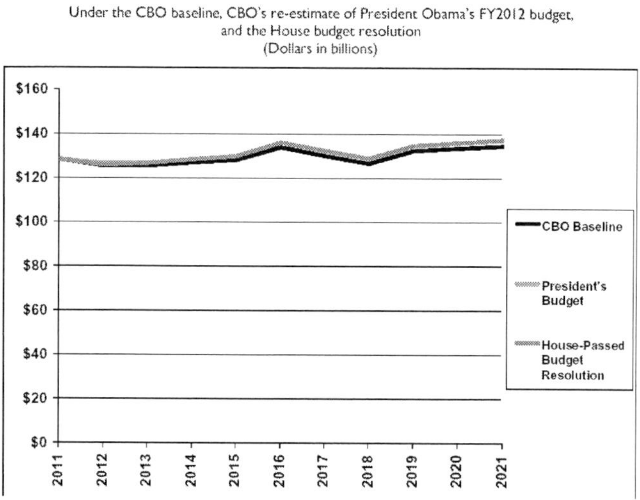

Source: Congressional Research Service (CRS), based on data from the Congressional Budget Office (CBO) and the House Budget Committee (HBC).

Notes: Inflation adjustment is based on the implicit price deflator for the Gross Domestic Product (GDP) based on CBO's forecast and projections. Outlays in FY2011 were estimated prior to enactment of the full-year continuing appropriations resolution, P.L. 112-10.

Figure 10. Federal Outlays for the Veterans Benefits and Service Budget Function, in Constant 2011 Dollars: FY2011 through FY2021.

Spending under this function is divided among five subfunctions:[32]

- income security for veterans;
- veterans education, training, and rehabilitation;
- hospital and medical care for veterans;
- veterans housing; and
- other veterans benefits and services.

Figure 10 shows estimated outlays for Function 700 programs, from FY2011 through FY2021 in constant FY2011 dollars, under the CBO baseline, the Administration's February budget request, and the House budget resolution. The Administration and House budgets for veterans benefits and services are virtually identical, and both very slightly exceed the CBO baseline.[33]

CONCLUSION

Programs categorized as "human resources" comprise the majority of federal outlays and have grown over the last five decades as a share of the overall national economy. CBO expects that spending for these programs will have peaked in FY2010 and will fall through FY2014, although spending levels will remain higher than they were before the recent recession. CBO further expects that overall human resources spending will begin to climb again starting in FY2015; however, all of the projected growth will be in health care (Medicaid and Medicare) and Social Security. All other components of the human resources superfunction will diminish as a share of the economy over the coming decade, according to CBO's current law baseline.

The Administration and Congress are engaged in a debate over reducing the federal deficit and stabilizing the national debt; proposals to reduce and change the composition of federal spending are a major part of this debate. In February, the Administration gave Congress a detailed budget request for FY2012, which includes proposals to reduce spending for certain programs and increase spending for others; the February budget request was followed in April with an additional set of deficit reduction principles. Based on an analysis of the February budget, the Administration proposes no overall reduction in outlays for the human resources superfunction, although some of the proposals included in the April *Framework* would further lower spending for this portion of the budget. The budget resolution passed in April by the House, on the other hand, sets spending targets that would reduce outlays in the human resources superfunction to a level that would be 14% below the CBO baseline by FY2021.

Within the human resources category, the House resolution would reduce spending primarily in three functions. By FY202 1, the resolution would result in spending for Function 500 (education, training, employment, and social services, or ETESS) that is 36% below the CBO baseline. The largest reduction from the CBO baseline, if all provisions in the House resolution were enacted, would occur in Function 550 (health, including Medicaid); the House spending target for this function in FY2021 would be 50% below the baseline. Finally, spending for Function 600 (income security) in FY2021 would be 11% below the baseline under the House resolution. As noted earlier in this report, most federal programs specifically directed to low-income populations are in the human resources superfunction and are most likely to be included in the three specific functions just mentioned.

In comparing these proposals, it is important to note the significant difference in size among the functions. For example, while the House budget resolution envisions a relatively large reduction in spending for Function 500 (ETESS) than would otherwise occur under current law, this proposal would contribute relatively little toward deficit reduction because of the small size of the function overall. On the other hand, with no change in current law CBO expects the function that includes Medicaid will be more than six times larger than Function 500 in FY2021 and the income security function will be more than four times larger; thus, reductions from the baseline in these functions would yield greater savings.

Although the House resolution assumes conversion of Medicare into a premium subsidy program, this would not take effect until FY2022, which is beyond the 10-year budget window and therefore not reflected in the spending trends displayed in this report. Likewise, neither the Administration's budget nor the House budget resolution includes specific changes to Social Security or veterans benefits and services. Social Security is currently the largest of the human resources functions under current law, and would remain so under both the Administration and House proposals, with projected spending in FY2021 that is 10 times that of Function 500 (ETESS) and more than twice that of Function 600 (income security). Projected Medicare spending would be more than seven times that of Function 500 in FY2021 and more than 50% larger than Function 600.

APPENDIX. TABLES

Table A-1. Federal Outlays for Human Resources Budget Functions as a Percent of GDP: FY2012-FY2021

Under the CBO baseline, President Obama's FY2012 budget, and the House budget resolution										
	2012	**2013**	**2014**	**2015**	**2016**	**2017**	**2018**	**2019**	**2020**	**2021**
ETESS (Function 500)										
CBO Baseline	0.68%	0.60%	0.57%	0.57%	0.58%	0.58%	0.57%	0.56%	0.54%	0.53%
President's Budget	0.75	0.63	0.61	0.60	0.60	0.60	0.58	0.57	0.55	0.53
House Budget Resolution	0.64	0.45	0.39	0.39	0.38	0.38	0.37	0.36	0.35	0.34
Change from CBO Baseline										
President's Budget	0.07	0.03	0.04	0.03	0.02	0.02	0.01	0.01	0.01	0.01
House Budget Resolution	-0.04	-0.15	-0.18	-0.19	-0.19	-0.20	-0.20	-0.20	-0.19	-0.19
Health (Function 550)										
CBO Baseline	2.28	2.25	2.54	2.81	3.00	3.10	3.14	3.22	3.28	3.36
President's Budget	2.31	2.27	2.54	2.79	2.98	3.05	3.09	3.17	3.23	3.30
House Budget Resolution	2.21	2.08	1.86	1.73	1.70	1.71	1.66	1.69	1.67	1.68
Change from CBO Baseline										
President's Budget	0.02	0.02	0.00	-0.01	-0.02	-0.05	-0.05	-0.05	-0.05	-0.07
House Budget Resolution	-0.07	-0.17	-0.68	-1.07	-1.30	-1.39	-1.48	-1.53	-1.60	-1.68
Medicare (Function 570)										
CBO Baseline	3.07	3.17	3.18	3.14	3.23	3.20	3.17	3.31	3.40	3.49
President's Budget	3.16	3.29	3.31	3.28	3.38	3.34	3.32	3.47	3.56	3.66
House Budget Resolution	3.07	3.17	3.19	3.15	3.24	3.19	3.14	3.26	3.32	3.40
Change from CBO Baseline										
President's Budget	0.08	0.11	0.13	0.14	0.14	0.14	0.15	0.16	0.16	0.17
House Budget Resolution	0.00	0.00	0.01	0.01	0.00	-0.01	-0.03	-0.05	-0.08	-0.09

Table A-1. (Continued)

	2012	2013	2014	2015	2016	2017	2018	2019	2020	2021
Income Security (Function 600)										
CBO Baseline	3.37	3.18	2.82	2.67	2.60	2.46	2.35	2.34	2.30	2.25
President's Budget	3.39	3.19	3.02	2.85	2.76	2.62	2.50	2.49	2.43	2.38
House Budget Resolution	3.19	2.97	2.64	2.36	2.29	2.17	2.07	2.08	2.04	2.01
Change from CBO Baseline										
President's Budget	0.02	0.00	0.20	0.17	0.16	0.16	0.15	0.14	0.14	0.13
House Budget Resolution	-0.18	-0.21	-0.18	-0.32	-0.30	-0.29	-0.28	-0.26	-0.25	-0.24
Social Security (Function 650)										
CBO Baseline	4.88	4.91	4.91	4.91	4.94	5.00	5.08	5.17	5.26	5.35
President's Budget	4.89	4.91	4.91	4.91	4.93	5.00	5.08	5.17	5.26	5.34
House Budget Resolution	4.88	4.90	4.91	4.91	4.93	5.00	5.08	5.17	5.26	5.34
Change from CBO Baseline										
President's Budget	0.01	0.00	0.00	0.00	0.00	-0.01	-0.01	-0.01	-0.01	-0.01
House Budget Resolution	0.00	0.00	0.00	0.00	0.00	-0.01	-0.01	-0.01	-0.01	-0.01
Veterans Benefits and Service (Function 700)										
CBO Baseline	0.81	0.78	0.77	0.75	0.76	0.72	0.68	0.69	0.68	0.67
President's Budget	0.82	0.79	0.78	0.76	0.77	0.73	0.69	0.71	0.70	0.69
House Budget Resolution	0.81	0.79	0.78	0.76	0.77	0.73	0.69	0.71	0.70	0.69
Change from CBO Baseline										
President's Budget	0.01	0.01	0.01	0.01	0.01	0.01	0.01	0.01	0.01	0.01
House Budget Resolution	0.00	0.01	0.01	0.01	0.01	0.01	0.01	0.01	0.01	0.01

	2012	2013	2014	2015	2016	2017	2018	2019	2020	2021
Total Human Resources										
CBO Baseline	15.10	14.90	14.79	14.86	15.10	15.05	14.99	15.30	15.46	15.65
President's Budget	15.31	15.08	15.17	15.19	15.42	15.33	15.26	15.56	15.72	15.90
House Budget Resolution	14.80	14.36	13.77	13.30	13.31	13.17	13.01	13.26	13.34	13.46
Change from CBO Baseline										
President's Budget	0.20	0.18	0.38	0.33	0.32	0.28	0.27	0.27	0.26	0.24
House Budget Resolution	-0.30	-0.53	-1.02	-1.56	-1.79	-1.88	-1.98	-2.04	-2.12	-2.20

Source: Congressional Research Service (CRS), based on data from the Congressional Budget Office (CBO) and the House Budget Committee (HBC).

Notes: GDP for FY2011 through FY2021 is based on CBO's forecasts and projections.

Table A-2. Federal Budget Authority for Human Resources Budget Functions: FY2012-FY2021

Under the CBO baseline, President Obama's FY2012 budget, and the House budget resolution (nominal dollars in millions)										
	2012	2013	2014	2015	2016	2017	2018	2019	2020	2021
ETESS (Function 500)										
CBO Baseline	92,170	96,253	100,772	106,408	113,450	118,547	120,926	123,294	125,228	127,437
President's Budget	107,785	100,681	106,163	110,943	117,863	121,741	123,533	125,410	126,767	128,562
House Budget Resolution	67,122	63,887	66,076	69,446	73,314	75,371	76,798	78,314	79,629	80,952
Change from CBO Baseline										
President's Budget	15,615	4,428	5,391	4,535	4,413	3,194	2,607	2,116	1,539	1,125
House Budget Resolution	-25,048	-32,366	-34,696	-36,962	-40,136	-43,176	-44,128	-44,980	-45,599	-46,485

Table A-2. (Continued)

	2012	2013	2014	2015	2016	2017	2018	2019	2020	2021
Health (Function 550)										
CBO Baseline	356,582	373,799	457,053	523,169	570,837	618,055	660,014	706,203	761,410	805,008
President's Budget	359,390	374,467	455,790	519,559	566,166	608,114	649,482	695,131	749,822	789,029
House Budget Resolution	341,873	343,733	338,064	327,012	320,409	339,663	349,840	371,826	395,908	404,674
Change from CBO Baseline										
President's Budget	2,808	668	-1,263	-3,610	-4,671	-9,941	-10,532	-11,072	-11,588	-15,979
House Budget Resolution	-14,709	-30,066	-118,989	-196,157	-250,428	-278,392	-310,174	-334,377	-365,502	-400,334
Medicare (Function 570)										
CBO Baseline	482,711	520,231	548,639	571,516	618,802	640,677	663,653	723,711	776,051	830,418
President's Budget	495,757	539,025	570,645	596,137	645,818	669,667	694,799	757,794	812,846	870,672
House Budget Resolution	481,521	519,903	550,105	573,252	618,945	637,938	657,067	711,486	758,271	809,106
Change from CBO Baseline										
President's Budget	13,046	18,794	22,006	24,621	27,016	28,990	31,146	34,083	36,795	40,254
House Budget Resolution	-1,190	-328	1,466	1,736	143	-2,739	-6,586	-12,225	-17,780	-21,312

	2012	2013	2014	2015	2016	2017	2018	2019	2020	2021
Income Security (Function 600)										
CBO Baseline	534,346	524,859	488,868	489,260	495,528	495,553	499,548	515,122	526,706	539,225
President's Budget	537,181	524,400	522,748	520,252	527,507	527,892	532,056	547,509	559,122	571,727
House Budget Resolution	501,664	487,498	457,308	431,150	436,659	436,985	441,467	457,183	468,308	480,687
Change from CBO Baseline										
President's Budget	2,835	-459	33,880	30,992	31,979	32,339	32,508	32,387	32,416	32,502
House-Passed Budget Resolution	-32,682	-37,361	-31,560	-58,110	-58,869	-58,568	-58,081	-57,939	-58,398	-58,538
Social Security (Function 650)										
CBO Baseline	769,468	808,220	851,456	898,521	949,770	1,007,309	1,070,010	1,136,723	1,207,667	1,279,766
President's Budget	770,184	808,309	851,373	898,097	948,919	1,006,070	1,068,530	1,135,040	1,205,787	1,277,695
House Budget Resolution	769,060	807,668	850,744	897,641	948,701	1,006,098	1,068,714	1,135,334	1,206,195	1,278,208
Change from CBO Baseline										
President's Budget	716	89	-83	-424	-851	-1,239	-1,480	-1,683	-1,880	-2,071
House Budget Resolution	-408	-552	-712	-880	-1,069	-1,211	-1,296	-1,389	-1,472	-1,558

Table A-2. (Continued)

	2012	2013	2014	2015	2016	2017	2018	2019	2020	2021
Veterans' Benefits and Services (Function 700)										
CBO Baseline	127,813	128,896	132,578	136,153	145,056	143,844	142,817	152,337	156,667	161,032
President's Budget	128,332	130,012	134,125	138,143	147,382	146,311	145,399	155,078	159,666	164,367
House Budget Resolution	128,339	130,024	134,143	138,167	147,410	146,323	145,412	155,091	159,680	164,381
Change from CBO Baseline										
President's Budget	519	1,116	1,547	1,990	2,326	2,467	2,582	2,741	2,999	3,335
House Budget Resolution	526	1,128	1,565	2,014	2,354	2,479	2,595	2,754	3,013	3,349
Total Human Resources										
CBO Baseline	2,363,090	2,452,258	2,579,366	2,725,027	2,893,443	3,023,985	3,156,968	3,357,390	3,553,729	3,742,886
President's Budget	2,398,629	2,476,894	2,640,844	2,783,131	2,953,655	3,079,795	3,213,799	3,415,962	3,614,010	3,802,052
House Budget Resolution	2,289,579	2,352,713	2,396,440	2,436,668	2,545,438	2,642,378	2,739,298	2,909,234	3,067,991	3,218,008
Change from CBO Baseline										
President's Budget	35,539	24,636	61,478	58,104	60,212	55,810	56,831	58,572	60,281	59,166
House Budget Resolution	-73,511	-99,545	-182,926	-288,359	-348,005	-381,607	-417,670	-448,156	-485,738	-524,878

Source: Congressional Research Service (CRS), based on data from the Congressional Budget Office (CBO) and the House Budget Committee (HBC).

Table A-3. Federal Outlays for Human Resource Budget Functions: FY2012-FY2021

Under the CBO baseline, President Obama's FY2012 budget, and the House budget resolution (nominal dollars in millions)										
	2012	**2013**	**2014**	**2015**	**2016**	**2017**	**2018**	**2019**	**2020**	**2021**
ETESS (Function 500)										
CBO Baseline	106,567	97,952	98,900	104,557	110,416	115,636	119,255	121,704	123,942	125,962
President's Budget	117,304	103,526	105,009	109,928	115,088	119,756	122,340	124,132	125,749	127,336
House Budget Resolution	100,012	73,071	68,044	70,450	73,310	75,665	77,013	78,385	79,806	81,047
Change from CBO Baseline										
President's Budget	10,737	5,574	6,109	5,371	4,672	4,120	3,085	2,428	1,807	1,374
House Budget Resolution	-6,555	-24,881	-30,856	-34,107	-37,106	-39,971	-42,242	-43,319	-44,136	-44,915
Health (Function 550)										
CBO Baseline	358,252	369,094	438,480	510,544	574,941	620,635	657,339	702,939	747,616	801,097
President's Budget	362,012	372,417	438,883	507,922	570,707	611,004	647,047	692,103	736,279	785,268
House Budget Resolution	346,636	340,608	320,444	315,117	325,200	342,703	347,303	368,558	382,056	400,682
Change from CBO Baseline										
President's Budget	3,760	3,323	403	-2,622	-4,234	-9,631	-10,292	-10,836	-11,337	-15,829
House Budget Resolution	-11,616	-28,486	-118,036	-195,427	-249,741	-277,932	-310,036	-334,381	-365,560	-400,415

Table A-3. (Continued)

	2012	2013	2014	2015	2016	2017	2018	2019	2020	2021
Medicare (Function 570)										
CBO Baseline	482,534	520,411	548,498	571,322	618,967	640,526	663,443	723,862	775,884	830,224
President's Budget	495,426	539,219	570,567	595,989	646,017	669,549	694,627	757,986	812,722	870,524
House Budget Resolution	481,816	520,406	550,248	573,333	619,385	638,059	657,111	711,897	758,376	809,201
Change from CBO Baseline										
President's Budget	12,892	18,808	22,069	24,667	27,050	29,023	31,184	34,124	36,838	40,300
House Budget Resolution	-718	-5	1,750	2,011	418	-2,467	-6,332	-11,965	-17,508	-21,023
Income Security (Function 600)										
CBO Baseline	529,437	522,322	486,303	486,504	497,139	492,819	492,052	512,130	523,731	536,240
President's Budget	532,169	523,134	521,431	517,774	528,613	524,402	523,673	543,386	554,836	567,211
House Budget Resolution	501,006	487,248	456,072	429,143	438,896	434,795	434,302	454,448	465,565	477,942
Change from CBO Baseline										
President's Budget	2,732	812	35,128	31,270	31,474	31,583	31,621	31,256	31,105	30,971
House Budget Resolution	-28,431	-35,074	-30,231	-57,361	-58,243	-58,024	-57,750	-57,682	-58,166	-58,298

	2012	2013	2014	2015	2016	2017	2018	2019	2020	2021
Social Security (Function 650)										
CBO Baseline	766,442	804,802	847,699	894,237	945,083	1,002,066	1,064,515	1,130,825	1,201,170	1,273,219
President's Budget	767,275	804,948	847,748	893,806	944,233	1,000,844	1,063,037	1,129,142	1,199,287	1,271,140
House Budget Resolution	766,217	804,387	847,118	893,490	944,153	1,000,980	1,063,315	1,129,525	1,199,780	1,271,743
Change from CBO Baseline										
President's Budget	833	146	49	-431	-850	-1,222	-1,478	-1,683	-1,883	-2,079
House Budget Resolution	-225	-415	-581	-747	-930	-1,086	-1,200	-1,300	-1,390	-1,476
Veterans' Benefits and Services (Function 700)										
CBO Baseline	126,850	128,704	132,442	135,895	144,585	143,287	142,212	151,719	156,049	160,373
President's Budget	127,972	130,013	134,037	137,827	146,840	145,692	144,738	154,394	158,965	163,608
House Budget Resolution	127,140	130,025	134,055	137,851	146,868	145,704	144,751	154,407	158,979	163,622
Change from CBO Baseline										
President's Budget	1,122	1,309	1,595	1,932	2,255	2,405	2,526	2,675	2,916	3,235
House Budget Resolution	290	1,321	1,613	1,956	2,283	2,417	2,539	2,688	2,930	3,249

Table A-3. (Continued)

	2012	2013	2014	2015	2016	2017	2018	2019	2020	2021
Total Human Resources										
CBO Baseline	2,370,082	2,443,285	2,552,322	2,703,059	2,891,131	3,014,969	3,138,816	3,343,179	3,528,392	3,727,115
President's Budget	2,402,158	2,473,257	2,617,675	2,763,246	2,951,498	3,071,247	3,195,462	3,401,143	3,587,838	3,785,087
House Budget Resolution	2,322,827	2,355,745	2,375,981	2,419,384	2,547,812	2,637,906	2,723,795	2,897,220	3,044,562	3,204,237
Change from CBO Baseline										
President's Budget	32,076	29,972	65,353	60,187	60,367	56,278	56,646	57,964	59,446	57,972
House Budget Resolution	-47,255	-87,540	-176,341	-283,675	-343,319	-377,063	-415,021	-445,959	-483,830	-522,878

Source: Congressional Research Service (CRS) based on data from the Congressional Budget Office (CBO) and the House Budget Committee (HBC).

End Notes

[1] See *The Moment of Truth: Report of the National Commission on Fiscal Responsibility and Reform*, at http://www.fiscalcommission.gov/news/moment-truth-report-national-commissi-on-fiscal-responsibility-and-reform. Also see CRS Report R41784, *Reducing the Budget Deficit: The President's Fiscal Commission and Other Initiatives* , by Mindy R. Levit; and CRS Report R41641, *Reducing the Budget Deficit: Tax Policy Options*, by Molly F. Sherlock.

[2] The text of these amendments can be found in U.S. Congress, House Rules Committee, report to accompany H.Res. 223, 112th Cong., 1st sess., April 13, 2011, H.Rept. 112-62 (Washington: GPO, 2011).

[3] See CRS Report 98-280, *Functional Categories of the Federal Budget*, by Bill Heniff Jr.

[4] See CRS Report 98-815, *Budget Resolution Enforcement*, by Bill Heniff Jr.

[5] These programs are referred to as automatic stabilizers. For a discussion, see *The Effects of Automatic Stabilizers on the Federal Budget*, by the Congressional Budget Office, April 2011: http://www.cbo.gov/doc.cfm?index=12129.

[6] American Recovery and Reinvestment Act of 2009 (ARRA, P.L. 111-5).

[7] Patient Protection and Affordable Care Act (PPACA, P.L. 111-148, as amended by P.L. 111-152).

[8] Notably, Social Security is a self-financed program, with income from three sources: payroll taxes paid by covered workers and their employers, federal income taxes paid by some beneficiaries on a portion of their benefits, and interest income from the Social Security trust fund investments. (See section on "Social Security Program Financing" in CRS Report RL33544, *Social Security Reform: Current Issues and Legislation*, by Dawn Nuschler.) Medicare is partially financed through a dedicated payroll tax; other sources of financing include beneficiary premiums and general revenues. (See CRS Report R41436, *Medicare Financing*, by Patricia A. Davis.)

[9] For identification and discussion of federal low-income programs, see CRS Report R41625, *Federal Benefits and Services for People with Low Income: Programs, Policy, and Spending, FY2008-FY2009*, by Karen Spar.

[10] This analysis can be found in CRS Report R41 823, *Low-Income Assistance Programs: Trends in Federal Spending*, by Gene Falk.

[11] See CRS Report R41778, *Reducing the Budget Deficit: Policy Issues*, by Marc Labonte; CRS Report R41784, *Reducing the Budget Deficit: The President's Fiscal Commission and Other Initiatives* , by Mindy R. Levit; and CRS Report R41641, *Reducing the Budget Deficit: Tax Policy Options*, by Molly F. Sherlock.

[12] For an analysis of this proposal, see CRS Report R41174, *Impact on the Federal Budget of Freezing Non-Security Discretionary Spending*, by Mindy R. Levit.

[13] See *The Moment of Truth: Report of the National Commission on Fiscal Responsibility and Reform*, at http://www.fiscalcommission.gov/news/moment-truth-report-national-commission- fiscal-responsibility-and-reform.

[14] The fact sheet does not identify which programs would be considered "low-income" for this purpose.

[15] House Budget Committee Chairman Ryan's Path to Prosperity says the budget resolution sets spending targets that are below the levels set by H.R. 1, which was the full-year FY2011 continuing appropriations resolution passed by the House in February and defeated by the Senate in March. See CRS Report R41703, *FY2011 Appropriations: A Side-bySide Comparison of Key Proposals*, coordinated by Garrett Hatch and Marian Leonardo Lawson.

[16] Under Section 302(a) of the Congressional Budget Act of 1974 (P.L. 93-344, as amended), discretionary spending allocations are made to the House and Senate Appropriations Committees, reflecting the discretionary spending targets established in the congressional budget resolution; under Section 302(b) of the Budget Act, these allocations are further

divided among each of the appropriations subcommittees. On May 11, 2011, House Appropriations Committee Chairman Rogers announced preliminary "302(b) allocations" to the subcommittees, reflecting the spending targets in H.Con.Res. 34, as passed by the House. They are available at http://republicans.appropriations.house.gov/files/51111FY2012SubcommitteeAllocations302bs.pdf.

[17] Budget function descriptions used in this report can be found on the House Budget Committee website: http://budget.house.gov/BudgetProcess/BudgetFunctions.htm.

[18] For long-term trends in discretionary spending for each of the Function 500 subfunctions, see Figure 2 in CRS Report R41726, *Discretionary Budget Authority by Subfunction: An Overview*, by D. Andrew Austin.

[19] For background, see CRS Report R41437, *Federal Pell Grant Program of the Higher Education Act: Background, Recent Changes, and Current Legislative Issues*, by Shannon M. Mahan.

[20] The vast majority of spending in Function 550 is mandatory, for Medicaid and CHIP. For long-term trends in *discretionary* spending for the health care services and health research and training subfunctions, see Figures 3 and 4 in CRS Report R41726, *Discretionary Budget Authority by Subfunction: An Overview*, by D. Andrew Austin.

[21] For an explanation of the Federal Medical Assistance Percentage (FMAP), which is the formula used to determine the federal and state shares of spending under Medicaid and CHIP, see CRS Report RL32950, *Medicaid: The Federal Medical Assistance Percentage (FMAP)*, by Evelyne P. Baumrucker and Alison Mitchell.

[22] For a more complete discussion of the House budget resolution's Medicaid and private health insurance proposals, see CRS Report R41767, *Overview of Health Care Changes in the FY2012 Budget Offered by House Budget Committee Chairman Ryan*, by Patricia A. Davis, Alison Mitchell, and Bernadette Fernandez.

[23] For the long-term trends in *discretionary* spending included in Function 570 (primarily Medicare administration), see Figure 3 in CRS Report R41726, *Discretionary Budget Authority by Subfunction: An Overview*, by D. Andrew Austin.

[24] For background, see CRS Report R40907, *Medicare Physician Payment Updates and the Sustainable Growth Rate (SGR) System*, by Jim Hahn.

[25] For background, see CRS Report R4151 1, *The Independent Payment Advisory Board*, by David Newman and Christopher M. Davis.

[26] For a more complete discussion of the House budget resolution's Medicare proposals, see CRS Report R41767, *Overview of Health Care Changes in the FY2012 Budget Offered by House Budget Committee Chairman Ryan*, by Patricia A. Davis, Alison Mitchell, and Bernadette Fernandez.

[27] The ACTC is a refundable credit, available to certain families who also qualify for the nonrefundable Child Tax Credit but whose tax liability is too low for them to fully benefit from the nonrefundable credit. The refundable portions of tax credits such as EITC and ACTC are recorded as outlays; the nonrefundable portions are considered tax expenditures.

[28] For long-term trends in discretionary spending for each of the subfunctions included in Function 600, see Figure 5 in CRS Report R41726, *Discretionary Budget Authority by Subfunction: An Overview*, by D. Andrew Austin.

[29] For long-term trends in discretionary spending for Social Security, see Figure 5 in CRS Report R41726, *Discretionary Budget Authority by Subfunction: An Overview*, by D. Andrew Austin.

[30] Most Social Security spending is "off-budget," which means it is not included in the annual congressional budget process. For an explanation, see the section titled "On-Budget Versus Off-Budget" in CRS Report RL33028, *Social Security: The Trust Fund*, by Dawn Nuschler and Gary Sidor.

[31] For a discussion of Social Security reform issues and current proposals, see CRS Report RL33544, *Social Security Reform: Current Issues and Legislation*, by Dawn Nuschler.

[32] For long-term trends in discretionary spending for each of the subfunctions included in Function 700, see Figure 5 in CRS Report R41726, *Discretionary Budget Authority by Subfunction: An Overview*, by D. Andrew Austin. The hospital and medical care subfunction is also displayed in Figure 4 of CRS Report R41726.

[33] For a discussion of the Administration's FY20 12 budget request for veterans' benefits and services, see CRS Report R41688, *Veterans Affairs: A Preliminary Analysis of the FY2012 Appropriations Request* , by Christine Scott and Sidath Viranga Panangala.

INDEX

D

E

F

G

H

T

U

V

W